RESEARCH IN
TRANSPORTATION
ECONOMICS

Volume 4 • 1996

RESEARCH IN TRANSPORTATION ECONOMICS

Editor: B. STARR McMULLEN
Department of Economics
Oregon State University

VOLUME 4 • 1996

 JAI PRESS INC.

Greenwich, Connecticut   *London, England*

ISBN: 1-55938-915-X
ISSN: 0739-8859

Manufactured in the United States of America

CONTENTS

LIST OF CONTRIBUTORS

David S. Bunch   Graduate School of Management
University of California, Davis

David Brownstone   Department of Economics
University of California, Irvine

Thomas F. Golob   Institute of Transportation Studies
University of California, Irvine

Eric L. Jessup   Department of Agricultural
Economics
Washington State University

Andrew N. Kleit   Department of Economics
Louisiana State University

Bruce H. Kobayashi   School of Law
George Mason University

Weiping Ren   Department of Economics
University of California, Irvine

Krista Richards   Department of Economics
Oregon State University

Ann Schwarz-Miller   Department of Economics
Old Dominion University

Wayne K. Talley   Department of Economics
Old Dominion University

Wesley W. Wilson   Department of Economics
University of Oregon

PREFACE

Volume 4 of *Research in Transportation Economics* includes articles on a variety of topics of interest to transportation economists. Reported research includes the investigation of market power with case studies from the airline and railroad industries, an analysis of labor union power in the transit industry, a model to forecast demand for alternative fuel vehicles, and a paper which examines how leniency in the enforcement of overweight truck violations leads to overutilization of the highway system.

The first three papers are concerned with issues related to market power and possible anti-competitive behavior. Kleit and Kobayashi address the question of whether slot markets at high density airports have resulted in the exercise of market power by dominant carriers serving those locations. In particular, it has been argued that large carriers hoard slots, allowing them to engage in anti-competitive pricing behavior. The authors develop hypotheses to examine whether airport slot usage is consistent with anti-competitive behavior or alternatively, whether efficient market behavior is indicated. Statistical results for Chicago O'Hare suggest that slot usage by dominant carriers reflects efficient utilization rather than exercise of monopoly power.

The paper by Richards explores the question of whether the presence or potential entry of a low cost air carrier affects average fares on a route. Past studies have shown a positive correlation between average fares and concentration on a route, suggesting the presence of market power. Although Richards finds concentration (measured by a Herfindahl Index) to be positively related to yield in a pooled regression, concentration has no effect on yield when explicit consideration is given to the presence or potential presence of a low cost rival on a route. In particular, routes either served by Southwest Airlines or on which Southwest Airlines serves one endpoint (making it a potential entrant), have significantly lower fares than comparable routes where Southwest is neither an actual or potential competitor. These results suggest that low cost carriers play an important role in curbing the exercise of market power.

The article by Wilson examines rail rates in markets where the railroad carrier was found to be "market dominant," as determined by the Interstate Commerce Commission (ICC). He develops a model of railroad pricing that links theory with regulatory practice and then uses the model to quantify the impact of competition on rates. Evidence from the McCarthy Farms Case, where the railroad was found to be "market dominant" in the provision of grain transportation services, is used for the empirical part of the study. Assuming that the Montana markets considered were in fact monopoly markets as decreed by the ICC, Wilson's results suggest that the presence of competitive pressures led to markdowns from the monopoly price of about 21.75 percent for barley and 40 percent for wheat.

The paper by Schwarz-Miller and Talley examines the issue of whether unionized transit labor has been able to obtain higher wages than those in closely related industries, such as intercity bus. It has been argued that transit subsidies led to inflated earnings for transit workers and that the 1980s movement towards privatization in the transit industry would reduce these inflated transit wages. The Schwarz-Miller and Talley study finds that prior to 1982 unionized transit driver wages were actually 10 percent less than those of unionized intercity bus drivers. Following 1982, however, the situation reversed itself and unionized transit drivers enjoyed a 6 percent wage premium over their unionized intercity bus counterparts. Further, they find that unionized transit wage after 1982 do not exceed those of non-transit unionized government employees. These results suggest that deregulation of the intercity bus industry reduced union bargaining power there more than the various Reagan administration moves towards privatization reduced the power of unionized transit labor.

Brownstone, Bunch, Golub, and Ren provide a forecasting framework in which to consider the demand for alternative fuel vehicles. This is an important issue in urban areas where there is increasing concern regarding the relationship between transportation and environmental concern, air quality in particular. The dynamic vehicle transactions model they have developed combines stated and revealed preference models to obtain forecasts of demand for electric, methanol, and compressed natural gas fueled automobiles. Their results suggest that the demand for alternative fueled vehicles could be up to 39 percent of total vehicle transactions with methanol and natural gas autos comprising about 35 percent of demand and electric vehicles only 4 percent.

The topic in transportation for this volume is a paper by Eric Jessup that examines the controversial issue of how to prevent overweight trucks that increase road damage. His case study of the Washington State system suggests that overweight trucks are encouraged by the failure of the judicial system to enforce the legally prescribed fees and fines. Thus the problem for policymakers is not simply to develop an optimal pricing system for overweight vehicles, but also to convince the judicial system that these fees cannot be reduced or waived without subverting their purpose.

The purpose of this publication is to promote and disseminate research related to transportation economics and policy. The six papers in this volume are indicative of the breadth and quality of work in transportation economics. It is expected that future volumes of *Research in Transportation Economics* will continue to include work on diverse aspects of transportation with economic analysis being the theme common to all research presented in this series.

B. Starr McMullen
Series Editor

MARKET FAILURE OR MARKET EFFICIENCY?

EVIDENCE ON AIRPORT SLOT USAGE

Andrew N. Kleit and Bruce H. Kobayashi

ABSTRACT

Beginning in 1986, the FAA has allowed the rights to take off or land at the four "High Density Traffic Airports" (HDTAs), known as "slots," to be sold or traded for any consideration. Opponents of this system have alleged that the slot markets are prone to various forms of "market failure." The main allegations have been that dominant carriers at the HDTAs have been "hoarding" slots in order to generate higher than competitive prices for airline services. This article attempts to test empirically the various anticompetitive hoarding hypotheses by examining slot ownership and usage data at the most concentrated HDTA, Chicago's O'Hare airport. In general, we find a positive and significant relationship between the

Research in Transportation Economics, Volume 4, pages 1-32.
Copyright © 1996 by JAI Press Inc.
All rights of reproduction in any form reserved.
ISBN: 1-55938-915-X.

rate at which a carrier uses a slot and the carrier's market share. This is consistent with a theory of efficient use of slots by carriers owning a large share of the slots at a HDTA. In addition, there is no evidence that the two largest carriers are using leasing as an anticompetitive device. On the other hand, our results concerning capacity usage are consistent with both hoarding and efficiency hypotheses. Taken as a whole, however, the statistical evidence presented here is more consistent with the hypothesis that efficiency considerations were generating concentration at O'Hare.

I. INTRODUCTION

Economists have long advocated the use of well defined and transferable property rights as the efficient solution to the problem of allocating common property resources. While there are some examples where market-based systems have been used as an alternative to direct governmental control to allocate common property resources, their widespread use has been successfully resisted by the political process—that is, even in areas where movement towards the use of market-based systems has been made, such as in the area of allocating rights to the broadcast spectrum[1] and the allocation of pollution rights,[2] the movement is far from complete.

One area in which the relatively unrestricted use of market forces is currently being used to reallocate resources is the Federal Aviation Administration's (FAA) regulation of take-off and landing rights at some of the most congested airports in the country.[3] Beginning in 1986, the FAA has allowed the rights to take off or land at the four "High Density Traffic Airports" (HDTAs), known as "slots," to be sold or traded for any consideration. While the creation of the right to buy and sell slots was designed to enhance economic efficiency, the use of market forces to reallocate landing rights has been subject to substantial controversy. Opponents of the market-based system have alleged that the slot markets are prone to various forms of "market failure." The main allegations have been that dominant carriers at the HDTAs have been "hoarding" slots in order to generate higher than competitive prices for airline services.

This article attempts to test empirically the various anticompetitive hoarding hypotheses by examining slot ownership and usage data at the most concentrated HDTA, Chicago's O'Hare airport. While our analysis concentrates on the variable of direct interest to regulatory authorities, slot usage, we also hope to address two other issues. First, we hope to shed light on a traditional question in industrial organization: Does concentration create anticompetitive behavior, or does efficiency create concentration? Our results are most consistent with the later hypothesis. Second, an analysis of the performance of the slot market can generate information as to the utility of expanding the use of marketable rights to other congested airports and to other areas of government regulation, such as the allocation of radio spectrum and the allocation of emission rights for pollution control.

The article is organized as follows. Section II discusses the background of the FAA slot rule, and discusses empirical implications of the anticompetitive hoarding and the procompetitive use hypotheses. Section III describes the data used in this analysis. Section IV empirically tests the hypotheses set out in Section II by examining slot usage as a function of market share. Section V concludes the article.

II. BACKGROUND

A. History

Slots were defined in 1968 in response to excess demand and noise considerations at the four HDTAs (Chicago's O'Hare, New York's LaGuardia and Kennedy, and Washington DC's National). Before 1985, reallocations of slots were subject to approval by committees consisting of all carriers who flew or wanted to fly into a particular airport. The default allocation, should no unanimous decision be forthcoming, was to keep the previous allocation in place. The post-1977 era of airline deregulation placed severe strains on this method, and the system broke down almost completely, freezing the existing allocation scheme in place.[4] This created a *de facto* absolute barrier to entry, as there was no method by which a new entrant could gain a slot at an HDTA.[5] After the 1981 air controllers strike, slot restrictions were imposed for a limited time on an additional 18 airports. For a six-week period in 1982, the FAA allowed slots to be traded and sold among airlines at these 22 airports.[6]

The FAA changed its regulation so that starting in April 1986 a market in slots could arise at the four HDTAs.[7] This decision was due in part to the failure of the committee system and to the apparent success of the six-week market following the controllers strike. Slot rights were "grandfathered," with the right to a particular slot going to whichever carrier previously had been operating that slot.[8] Slots were tradeable and leasable for any consideration and any party could own a slot. In addition, the FAA placed "use or lose" restrictions on slots, that is, a carrier must forfeit a slot if it is used less than 65 percent of the time.

Each slot was randomly assigned a withdrawal number. The withdrawal number denotes the order in which a slot for a given time period is subjèct to withdrawal from carriers by the FAA, with the lowest numbered slots being the first ones to be withdrawn. Withdrawn slots are generally allocated to international flights, although the FAA has made it clear it has the option of withdrawing slots and reallocating them for competitive purposes.[9]

B.   Theory and Hypotheses

The use of market-based systems to transfer slots has generated significant opposition. Commentators have suggested that the slot markets have not evolved competitively, and that the large carriers have used the slot market to acquire and maintain market power at the HDTAs. These commentators have pointed to higher concentration and prices for airline travel at HDTAs relative to non-HDTA airports as evidence of a lack of competition at HDTAs. For example, estimates of the effect of limited slot availability on airfares suggest that slot restrictions increase average or median fares eleven percent on short haul routes, and four percent for all routes to and from the HDTAs.[10] There also has been a focus on the levels of concentration at the HDTAs.[11]

Table 1 lists the unrestricted air carrier slot holdings and the Herfindahl-Hirschmann Index (HHI) of concentration at the four HDTA's as of June 30, 1990. New York's LaGuardia, at 1241, and Washington's National, at 1282, were "moderately concentrated," according to the standards of the Department of Justice (DOJ) Merger Guidelines.[12] New York's Kennedy, at 1816, and Chicago's O'Hare, at 3122, were "highly concentrated."

Concentrated markets for airport slots could create conditions for the exercise of market power or other anticompetitive action.[13] It should be noted, however, that neither higher concentration nor higher prices at HDTAs necessarily implies anticompetitive effects or causes. First, economic theory predicts that in competitive markets, fares at slot constrained airports will be higher, *ceteris paribus*, than in markets where there are no slot restrictions. Equilibrium competitive prices for air travel must reflect slots' associated scarcity rents. Indeed, if travel prices were not higher at slot constrained airports, this would imply that landing rights at HDTAs were not a valuable resource, so slots would not trade at positive prices. Higher fares at HDTAs may thus merely reflect scarcity rents, rather than monopoly profits.

Second, there may be a procompetitive reason for seemingly high concentration in airport slot markets: in competitive markets, more efficient firms, which offer their customers better combinations of price and service, generally gain market share at the expense of less efficient firms.[14] That is, an industry might be relatively concentrated because its larger firms are more efficient, not because they are less competitive. Thus, it is possible that only a few airlines hold a majority of the slots as a consequence of those carriers' greater efficiency. In effect, it may be that efficiency is causing concentration, instead of concentration causing anticompetitive behavior.

Finally, the concentration figures for HDTAs may overstate the potential for anticompetitive activity because they do not describe antitrust markets. In antitrust analysis, before concentration is measured markets must be defined. A concentration number for something that is not an antitrust market, that does not include relevant product and geographic competitive factors, will be misleading. Each of the HDTAs is near one or more regional

Table 1. Domestic Slot Holdings and Concentration
Unrestricted Slots, 6-30-90

Slot Holder	LaGuardia (LGA) #	Share of Slots	National (DCA) #	Share of Slots	Kennedy (JFK) #	Share of Slots	O'Hare (ORD) #	Share of Slots
United	45	7.28	28	4.87	6	3.11	658	44.25
American	57	9.22	35	6.09	21	10.88	491	33.02
USAIR	151	24.43	148	25.74	20	10.36	45	3.03
Eastern[1]	72	11.65	82	14.26	17	8.81	21	1.41
Northwest	45	7.28	53	9.22	12	6.22	71	4.77
Delta	56	9.06	47	8.17	9	4.66	64	4.37
Shawmut Bank[2]	24	3.88	44	7.65	60	31.09	36	2.42
Pan Am	64	10.36	38	6.61	42	21.76	4	0.27
Continental	29	4.69	48	8.35	0	0	36	2.42
Trump	57	9.22	28	4.87	0	0	0	0
Air Wisconsin[3]	0	0	0	0	0	0	44	2.96
Midway	14	2.27	16	2.78	0	0.52	0	0
Amer. West	0	0	4	0.7	1	0	7	0.47
Midwest Exp.	4	0.65	4	0.7	0	0	2	0.13
Other	0	0	0	0	5	2.61	3	0.2
FAA	49					9		1
N	667		575		202		1488	
HHI	1241		1282		1816		3122	

Notes: [1] Although Eastern and Continental were merged in 1986, control of Eastern was taken away from Texas Air (Continental's parent entity) by a Federal bankruptcy court on April 18, 1990. We therefore threat Eastern and Continental as separate carriers.
[2] This bank held slots formerly held by TWA.
[3] As discussed in Section III, it is possible to consider United and Air Wisconsin as one carrier. If this assumption is used, the HHI at O'Hare increases 262 points to 3384.

Source: Tabulated from FAA Slot Data, May-June 1990.

airports without slot constraints (Midway at Chicago, Newark at New York, and Dulles and Baltimore-Washington International at Washington). If flights from these airports are in the same antitrust market as flights from the HDTAs,[15] their competitive presence can constrain the prices of flights from the HDTAs.[16]

In sum, the possibility of other reasons for both high prices and high concentration at HDTAs limits the usefulness of these variables alone to inform public policy decisions. To avoid the ambiguities of tests using price effects, our empirical work uses measures of output, rather than price, in an attempt to differentiate between procompetitive and anticompetitive uses of slots.[17] That is, the hypotheses tested here all derive from theoretical predictions about the output-setting choices made by relatively large firms compared to those of smaller firms. The first hypothesis to be tested rests on the standard market power scenario, in which dominant firms have a larger incentive to reduce output than the fringe firms. Standard theory predicts that the fringe will increase output in response to a contraction of output by the dominant firm (Alchian & Allen, 1983). In the context of an airport slot market, this implies that larger carriers will use their slots less intensively than the smaller "fringe" carriers. Conversely, if slots are being used efficiently, the larger carriers' slot usage would be as great or greater than slot usage by smaller carriers. The testable implication of such a procompetitive theory is that slot usage will be positively related to the market share of the carrier using the slot. In contrast, the anticompetitive theory implies the reverse, that is, that the dominant or colluding carriers will use their slots less than the competitive fringe.[18] Our test will measure the net effect, that is, whether or not the anticompetitive or the efficiency effect has the greatest impact on output.

Another form of the anticompetitive hypothesis is that dominant carriers would be unwilling to sell slots to potential new entrants at competitive rates,[19] but instead would lease slots to selected other carriers, their purpose being to deter entry into HDTAs by carriers likely to increase overall slot use.[20] The testable implications of this hypothesis are that the dominant air carriers will be net lessors of slots and that these leased slots will be used relatively less intensively than slots held and operated by the dominant carriers (see U.S. General Accounting Office, 1990, chap 2).

Finally, we must choose a measure of slot output. The claim that carriers with a large number of slots at a HDTA will attempt to restrict output by reducing the number of days on which a slot is used suggests using days a slot was operated as the measure of output. A hypothetical monopolist also could reduce slot output by operating smaller planes. Since slot use and aircraft size are complements, a hypothetical monopolist would be expected to reduce output on both margins. This permits us to examine both of these measures individually. Examining slot output by days used has the additional advantage on focusing on the measure of output that is the FAA's regulatory choice instrument. Part A of Section IV uses the number of days the slot was used as the measure of slot output. Part B of Section IV uses a measure of plane capacity (the number of seats used in the slot's aircraft operations) as the measure of slot output. We note, however, that interpretation of results of Part B will pose difficulties.[21]

III. THE DATA

The data were obtained from the FAA's Office of Slot Administration. The FAA collects daily ownership and usage data for monitoring airline compliance with ownership and usage rules. The slot office keeps this data for the two previous years, thus limiting the time periods available for examination. Data from the period May-June 1990 were chosen because it lies between the extremes of airlines' seasonal demands. May and June generally have lower demand for air travel than July and August and higher demand than January and February. In addition, May-June 1990 was after the time period when Eastern Airlines was unable to operate a large proportion of its planes due to the strike by its employees in March 1989. May-June 1990 was also prior to the August 1990 Iraqi invasion of Kuwait and the resulting decline in demand for air services. This time period consists of 44 weekdays and 61 days in total.

Data from O'Hare was chosen because O'Hare is the most concentrated HDTA and is also the only HDTA that is primarily used as a hub (by American and United). The high concentration might suggest that the potential for anticompetitive behavior would be greatest at O'Hare. The most likely hypothesis for the exercise of market power at O'Hare would involve tacit collusion between United (with a market share of 44.25 percent) and American (with a market share of 33.02 percent). On the other hand, the fact that O'Hare is the only HDTA used primarily as a hub suggests that efficiency-based theories may better explain its concentration level.

The original dataset contains 2,242 total slots at O'Hare. Statistical analysis is based on the set of slots meeting three criteria: (1) the slot was held and operated by a domestic airline on a domestic route; (2) use of the slot was not restricted by the FAA; and (3) the slot was not exempt from the FAA's "use or lose" rules. (International routes, and thus foreign airlines, are subject to different slot allocation rules.) This set contains 1,488 slots.[22]

We note one conceptual problem with the data. Although Air Wisconsin was independently owned and operated during the period studied and competed directly with United on a number of routes, it had a "code sharing" arrangement with United (i.e., it agreed to a large number of joint fares with United and was listed in the Official Airline Guide and on Computer Reservation Systems as UA*) and was subsequently purchased by United. We will therefore conduct our statistical tests using both the assumption that Air Wisconsin was an independent carrier and the assumption that Air Wisconsin was a part of United Airlines.

IV. EMPIRICAL RESULTS

A. Results Based on Days Used

Average Slot Use

Table 2 shows the average slot use by carrier measured by the proportion of total days used and weekdays used.[23] This data does

Table 2.   Average Slot Use
Average use rates below 90 percent in **bold.**

		All Days		Weekdays Only	
Slot Holder	#	Use Rate	Rate Fraction	Use Rate	Rate Fraction
America West	7	61.00	1.000	44.00	1.000
Eastern	21	59.05	0.968	42.67	0.970
Pan Am	4	57.50	0.943	41.75	0.949
Delta	64	57.30	0.939	42.17	0.958
United	658	57.25	0.939	42.48	0.966
American	491	56.51	0.926	41.08	0.934
Air Wisconsin	44	56.41	0.925	42.68	0.970
USAir	45	55.07	0.903	41.67	0.947
Flying Tiger	3	56.33	0.924	40.00	0.909
Continental	36	55.97	0.918	41.14	0.935
Shawmut Bank	36	55.81	0.915	41.03	0.932
Midwest Express	2	55.50	0.910	**38.50**	**0.875**
Northwest	71	54.90	0.900	41.24	0.937
FAA	1	**54.00**	**0.885**	**39.00**	**0.886**
American Trans	5	**49.20**	**0.807**	39.60	0.900
TOTAL	1488	56.77	0.931	41.87	0.951

Source: Tabulated from FAA Slot Data, May-June 1990.

not suggest that the intensity of use of a slot is negatively related to the share of slots held by the carrier, as the anticompetitive hypothesis would imply. Almost all of the slot holders use their slots on average at least 90 percent of the time, with United operating its slots 93.9 percent and American 92.6 percent. The only exceptions are American Trans Air, based on all days, and Midwest Express, based on weekdays. Even the slot holder with the lowest average use rate, American Trans Air at 80.7 percent, is 15.7 percentage points above the then existing FAA minimum use requirement of 65 percent.[24]

After the period of our data set, the FAA increased the minimum use or lose threshold from 65 percent to 80 percent.[25] Examination of the data suggests that such a rule will not have a large effect on the operations or slot holdings of the large carriers at O'Hare. All carriers, on average, would comply with the 80 percent rule. Further, the rule likely has little effect on the largest carriers at O'Hare. Based on the existing pattern of slot use during the May and June of 1990, application of the new 80 percent use or lose rule would have affected only two United slots and two American slots. Furthermore, these carriers could have easily reduced the number of affected slots by shifting flights from adjacent time periods, as allowed under the slot rules.[26] By performing this type of scheduling change, the leading carriers at O'Hare could have eliminated completely the effect of the new 80 percent use or lose rule. Similar results hold for the other slot holders at O'Hare.[27]

Leased Versus Owned Slots

Table 3 compares owned and operated slots with leased slots. The first and second columns of the table show each slot holder's rate of use of its owned and operated (O&O) slots, and the third and fourth columns show the rate of use of its slots that are used by others. Table 3 also denotes statistically significant differences in the rate of use between each slot holder's O&O slots and its slots leased to others.

The anticompetitive leasing hypothesis implies that this difference should be positive, that is, that the slot holder's O&O slots would be used at a higher rate than the slots leased to others. Examining the Table, we see that this is not the case for the three largest airlines at O'Hare. Based on weekday usage, the two largest airlines (in terms of slot market share) lease to carriers who use the slots at an equal or higher rate than do the lessors, with the difference being statistically significant for American. Based on all-days usage, the slots United leases to others are used slightly more than United's O&O slots, but the difference is not significant. The slots American leases to others are used at the same rate as its O&O slots. Contrary to the prediction of the anticompetitive leasing theory, it is the carriers with smaller slot shares, rather than the larger ones, that are more likely to use their O&O slots more intensively.

In addition, Table 3 lists the net leasing positions of specific carriers. The anticompetitive leasing hypothesis predicts that carriers with a large share of the slots at an HDTA will tend to

Table 3. Rates of Use in Owned and Operated Vs. Leased Slots

Leasing Slot Holder	All Days				Weekdays				Net Position
	N	O&O	Leased	Diff.	N	O&O	Leas.	Diff.	
United	639	0.940	0.942	-.002	9	0.966	0.970	-.004	20
American	411	0.928	0.928	.000	44	0.931	0.960	-.029*	34
Northwest	33	0.858	0.942	-.084*	33	0.929	0.946	-.017	-16
Delta	39	0.942	0.929	.013	21	0.970	0.935	.035*	-12
USAir	36	0.902	0.902	.000	6	0.954	0.909	.045*	1
Continental	17	0.934	0.899	.035	18	0.958	0.909	.049*	2
Eastern	12	0.993	0.934	.059*	9	0.998	0.932	.066*	-8

Notes: * Statistically significant at the 0.05 level using a two-tailed test. The test statistics were calculated using both the assumptions of equal and unequal variances.
Diff. equals the owned and operated use rate minus the leased use rate.
Net leasing position equals Slots operated − Slots held. Other net leasing positions were Air Wisconsin, 1; Shawmut Bank, -36; TWA, 27; America West, 0; American Trans Air, -5; Pan Am, -2; Flying Tiger, -3; Midwest Express, -2; FAA, -1.

be net lessors, so the hypothesis would be supported if the difference between the number of slots operated and the number of slots held is negative. The data show otherwise. Instead, the carriers with relatively large slot shares are almost always net lessees. At O'Hare, the carrier with the largest number of slots, United, leases 20 more slots from others than others lease from United; for the second largest, American, the comparable figure is 34.

A further examination of the leading carrier's net leasing position vis à vis individual airlines is also inconsistent with the anticompetitive leasing hypothesis. United leased only 9 of its slots for use by others; 6 to American, 2 to Delta, and 1 to Air Wisconsin. This would not appear to be enough to engage in any type of systematic anticompetitive leasing behavior. In addition, of the 29 slots leased by United from others, 6 slots each are leased from American (resulting in United having an even net leasing position with American) and Delta (result in United being a net lessee of 4 slots with Delta). Thus, the single slot leased to Air Wisconsin, United's code sharing airline, represents the only case in which United was a net lessor of slots.

Regression Analysis

A multiple regression setting was also used to examine the anticompetitive and competitive hypotheses. In these regressions, the dependent variable is the number of days a slot was used. The dependent variable is measured either by using all 61 days in the period or only the 44 weekdays. To test the anticompetitive usage hypothesis—that slots held by carriers with a large share of the slots at an HDTA will be used less intensively than slots held by carriers with a small slot share—against the procompetitive hypothesis, which suggests the opposite, the slot holder's share of slots at an HDTA was included as an independent variable. To examine the anticompetitive leasing hypothesis—that carriers with relatively more slots will lease their slots to carriers that use them at lower rates—a dummy variable that denotes whether or not a slot was leased and a variable that interacts this dummy variable with the slot share variable were included as independent variables.

To control for other factors that may affect slot use, dummy variables that denote whether a slot was held or was operated by more than one carrier during the time period, along with variables that interact these dummy variables with slot market share, were included as independent variables. To control for differences in use in peak versus off-peak periods, dummy variables that denote the beginning of the relevant time period were included as independent variables. Finally, the slot withdrawal number was included as an independent variable to control for possible differences in the strength of the property right associated with holding a slot.[28] The following linear specification was estimated using Tobit procedures:[29]

$$\text{DAYS OPERATED} = \alpha_0 + \alpha_1 \text{SLOT SHARE}$$
$$+ \alpha_2 \text{WITHDRAWAL PRIORITY} + \alpha_3 \text{LEASE}$$
$$+ \alpha_4 \text{LEASE*SLOT SHARE} + \alpha_5 \text{MULTIPLE OPERATOR}$$
$$+ \alpha_6 \text{MULTIPLE OPERATOR*SLOT SHARE}$$
$$+ \alpha_7 \text{MULTIPLE HOLDER}$$
$$+ \alpha_8 \text{MULTIPLE HOLDER*SLOT SHARE} + \alpha_t P_t + \Sigma\, \alpha_t P_t + \epsilon$$

where

DAYS OPERATED is the number of days (or weekdays) the slot was operated in the two month period,

SLOT SHARE is the slot holder's share of the total number of nonrestricted and nonexempt slots at the end of the two-month period,

WITHDRAWAL PRIORITY is the FAA withdrawal priority number,

LEASE is a dummy variable that equals one if the slot is operated by a single operator other than the slot holder, zero otherwise (slots held by Shawmut Bank and operated by TWA were not counted as leased).

MULTIPLE OPERATOR[30] is a dummy variable that equals one if the slot is operated by more than one operator, and was not traded in the two month period, zero otherwise,

MULTIPLE HOLDER is a dummy variable that equals one if the slot holder changed during the two month period,

P_t is a dummy variable that equals one if the slot's hour or half-hour period starts at time t. The dummy variable for the latest slot period is left out.

The anticompetitive usage hypothesis—that carriers with a large share of the slots at an HDTA will use their slots less intensively than carriers with a small slot share—is H_0: ∂NUMBER OF DAYS OPERATED/∂SLOT SHARE < 0, and the procompetitive hypothesis is H_1: ∂NUMBER OF DAYS OPERATED/∂SLOT SHARE ≥ 0. The anticompetitive leasing hypothesis— that carriers with a large slot share will lease their slots to carriers who will use these slots at a lower rate—is H_0: $\alpha_3 + \alpha_4$SLOT SHARE < 0 for SLOT SHARE large, and the procompetitive hypothesis again implies the opposite.

Table 4 reports regression results assuming that United and Air Wisconsin were separately operated (columns one and three) and assuming they were one carrier (columns two and four).[31] In general, the results do not support either anticompetitive hypothesis, regardless of which assumption regarding the independence of Air Wisconsin is used. Examining the regressions, the anticompetitive usage hypothesis can be rejected for the all-days regression. The direct coefficient on slot market share is positive and statistically significant, and the derivative of number of days operated with respect to slot market share is equal to 3.18 when the lease, multiple operator, and multiple holder variables are evaluated at their average values.[32] The anticompetitive usage hypothesis is also rejected by the weekday-only regressions. The weekdays regression implies that the derivative of number of weekdays used with respect to slot share equals 1.95 with the dummy variables evaluated at their average values. This in turn

Table 4. Regression Results
Dependent Variable — Number of Days Operated, May-June 1990
(t-statistics in parenthesis)

Variable	Coefficients			
	All Days		Weekdays Only	
	UA/AW Separate	UA/AW Together	UA/AW Separate	UA/AW Together
CONSTANT	50.43**	50.02**	38.29**	37.49**
	(5.19)	(5.22)	(3.60)	(4.10)
SLOT SHARE	4.32**	4.40**	2.44**	3.67**
	(5.04)	(5.12)	(3.64)	(5.48)
WITHDRAWAL PRI.	.0005*	.0005*	.0005**	.0006**
	(1.86)	(1.85)	(2.69)	(2.89)
LEASE	0.81	0.95*	-0.67	-0.16
	(1.49)	(1.70)	(-1.60)	(-0.37)
LEASE*SL. SH.	-3.54	-3.47	2.65	1.40
	(-1.50)	(-1.50)	(1.44)	(0.78)
MULT. OPERATOR	-2.07**	-1.93**	-1.49**	-1.00
	(-2.49)	(2.29)	(-2.33)	(-1.56)
MULT. OP.* SL. SH.	-0.63	-0.83	-0.37	-1.56
	(-0.20)	(-0.27)	(-0.15)	(-0.66)
MULTIPLE HOLD.	3.36	6.49	2.73	3.05
	(1.47)	(0.76)	(1.53)	(0.47)
MULT. HOLD.* SLOT SHARE	-16.54**	-19.17	-9.45*	-7.82
	(-2.42)	(-0.98)	(-1.77)	(-0.53)
N	1483	1483	1483	1483
MEAN DEP. VAR.	56.90	56.90	41.96	41.96
LOG LIKELIHOOD	-3513	-3514	-2774	-2766
% NON-EXTREME OBSERVATIONS	78.6%	78.6%	63.7%	63.7%

Notes: * Significant at the .05 level (one-tailed test).
          ** Significant at the .025 level (one-tailed test).

implies that, all other things being equal, a slot moving from Continental (with a 2.42 percent slot share) to United (with a slot share of 44.25 percent) would be used 1.33 days more during a two-month period, and 0.82 weekdays more.

Examining the anticompetitive leasing hypothesis, the coefficients on the lease dummy variable (α_3) and on the lease dummy interacted with slot market share (α_4), are mixed in sign, and none of the negative coefficients are statistically significant. The all days regression results imply that leased slots will be used more intensively than the lessor's owned and operated slots if the lessor's slot holding share is above 23 percent. That is, according to the regression results, the two largest carriers at O'Hare, United and American, would lease slots to carriers that use them at rates greater than or equal to the rate at which United and American use their owned and operated slots.[33]

As for the other variables, the coefficients on the variables denoting whether a slot changes operators suggest that these slots are used less. Similarly, the coefficients on the variable that denotes whether a slot had more than one owner during the period studied suggest that these slots were used less. The coefficient on the withdrawal number is positive and is statistically significant, possibly reflecting the assignment of highly valued or profitable flights to those slots least likely to be withdrawn (i.e., those with the highest withdrawal numbers). The sign of interaction term of the multiple operator dummy and slot share is mixed, but is not statistically significant in any regression. For expositional convenience, the coefficients on the time dummy variable are not reported. (Estimates of these coefficients are available upon request.) Overall, all regressions are statistically significant at the 1 percent level.

In general, the regression results for O'Hare based on slot usage support the procompetitive hypotheses. There is a positive and statistically significant relationship between slot share and rate of use. In addition, the regression based on weekdays suggests that slots leased by large carriers to others are used at a higher rate than their O&O slots. Both results are inconsistent with the anticompetitive hypotheses.

Table 5.   Capacity By Operating Carrier

Slot Holder	N	Average Daily Capacity per Slot	
		All Days	Weekdays Only
America West	7	239	239
Eastern	21	194	195
Pan Am	4	174	176
Flying Tiger	3	172	171
Midwest Express	2	169	166
American Trans Air	5	150	166
American	491	166	167
Shawmut Bank/TWA	36	157	160
Northwest	71	152	157
Delta	64	143	145
Continental	36	143	145
United	658	140	144
USAir	45	125	132
Air Wisconsin	44	102	106
TOTAL	1487	150	153

Source: Tabulated from FAA daily slot data, May 1-June 30, 1990.

B.   Results Using Number of Seats

The data on utilization rates measured by the number of days used do not suggest that large carriers hoard slots anticompetitively. Nonuse, however, is not the only potential means by which output can be restricted. For example, it has been claimed that the major airlines will fly smaller planes to hoard slots, that is, they will reduce the capacity or otherwise find a lower valued use for the slot than would an alternative carrier (e.g., by using the flight for a low valued destination), see U.S. General Accounting Office (1990).

In this section, we examine this claim by analyzing the capacity of the plane used with each slot. Table 5 lists average number of seats per slot day by carrier. Five small carriers (with 21 or fewer slots at O'Hare) have the largest average daily capacity per slot, with America West using solely Boeing 757s that list at 239 seats. Of the larger carriers at O'Hare, American flew the most seats per slot-day, 166, while TWA and Northwest were close behind at 157 and 152. In the middle of the seat rankings are Delta and

Continental, each at 143 seats per day, and United at 140 seats per day. The carriers flying the fewest number of seats per slot-day were USAir and Air Wisconsin, with 125 and 102 seats per slot-day.

Table 6 replicates Table 3, replacing slot usage with average daily capacity per slot holder. Table 6 indicates that there is no significant difference in capacity between United's leased and owned slots. In contrast, American (the second largest carrier) and Eastern (the smallest carrier with both owned and operated and leased slots) used their owned and operated slots at a significantly higher seat per day average than do their lessees. Examining the other slot holders, slots owned and operated by Delta, USAir, and Continental are used at a significantly lower seat per day average than slots leased from these carriers. (As noted above in Part A, the small number of slots United leases out makes the existence of the anticompetitive leasing hypothesis unlikely.)

Table 7 lists the results from running regressions using the average number of seats per day as the dependent variable. In the regressions where United and Air Wisconsin are treated as separate airlines, the coefficients on market share are generally negative, but are small and not statistically significant. The lease interaction term is negative and significant. The derivative of seat capacity with respect to slot share, with the dummy variables evaluated at their mean values, equals -6.96 for the all days regression and -8.87 for the weekday only regressions.

When Air Wisconsin and United are combined, however, the coefficient on market share becomes negative and statistically significant, the multiple holder interaction term becomes negative and statistically significant, and the multiple operator interaction term becomes positive and statistically significant. The derivative of seat capacity with respect to slot share, with the dummy variables evaluated at their mean values, equals -44.5 for the all days regression and -45.02 for the weekday only regressions. (Again, the coefficients for the slot period fixed effects are omitted for expositional convenience.) This in turn implies that, all other things being equal, a slot moving from Continental (with a 2.42 percent slot share) to United (with a slot share of 47.21 percent

Table 6. Average Daily Capacity of Owned and Operated Versus Leased Slots

	All Days				Weekdays Only			
	N	O&O	Leased	Diff.	N	'O&O	Leased	Diff.
United	639	140	146	-6	9	143	150	-7
American	412	170	130	40*	44	171	133	38*
Northwest	33	143	160	-17	33	152	160	-8
Delta	39	127	171	-44*	21	130	171	-41*
USAir	36	117	171	-54*	6	123	174	-51*
Continental	17	118	165	-47*	18	122	165	-43*
Eastern	12	212	169	43*	9	213	169	44*

Notes: * Statistically significant at the 0.05 level using a two-tailed test.
Diff. = O&O capacity level − Leased capacity level.

Source: Tabulated from FAA slot data, May-June 1990.

20

Table 7.   Regression Results
Dependent Variable — Average Daily Capacity, May-June 1990
(*t*-statistics in parenthesis)

| | Coefficients | | | |
| | All Days | | Weekdays Only | |
Variable	UA/AW Separate	UA/AW Together	UA/AW Separate	UA/AW Together
CONSTANT	247.05**	271.62**	255.18**	278.44**
	(13.50)	(14.98)	(13.87)	(15.28)
SLOT SHARE	**-0.13**	**-40.48****	**-3.65**	**-41.66****
	(-0.02)	**(-5.31)**	**(-0.47)**	**(-5.44)**
WITH. PRI.	-0.01**	-0.02**	-0.01**	-0.02**
	(-6.54)	(-7.15)	(-6.49)	(-7.06)
LEASE	15.44**	0.28	12.24**	-2.13
	(3.07)	(0.06)	(2.42)	(-0.42)
LEASE*SL.SH.	**-84.04****	**-40.72***	**-74.07****	**-33.26**
	(-3.88)	**(-1.94)**	**(-3.41)**	**(-1.58)**
MULT. OP.	-0.62	-15.94**	2.31	-12.26
	(-0.08)	(-2.08)	(0.30)	(-1.59)
MULT. OP.*SLOT SHARE	**31.76**	**72.54****	**36.85**	**75.56****
	(1.08)	**(2.54)**	**(1.25)**	**(2.64)**
MULT. HO.	-33.32	167.93**	-42.68**	178.46
	(-1.62)	(2.11)	(-2.06)	(2.24)
MULT. HO.*SLOT SHARE	**69.69**	**-410.57****	**106.59***	**-432.16****
	(1.11)	**(-2.28)**	**(1.70)**	**(-2.39)**
N	1483	1483	1483	1483
MEAN DEP. VR.	150.10	150.10	152.87	152.87
R-SQUARED	0.15	0.17	0.14	0.16
ADJ R-SQ.	0.13	0.15	0.12	0.14
F	7.05	8.11	6.42	7.48
LOG LIKEL.	-7488.78	-3513.28	-7496.00	-2774.65

Notes: * Significant at the .05 level (one-tailed test).
         ** Significant at the .025 level (one-tailed test).

in this specification) would have 19.71 seats less per day and 19.48 seats less per weekday.

Interpretation of such results are difficult. As noted above, use of smaller planes does not necessarily imply anticompetitive behavior. Due to the operating characteristics of aircraft, it may be more efficient to use smaller planes on shorter routes. In an efficient slot market, passengers on shorter routes with smaller planes will pay an additional premium to represent the higher per-passenger rent associated with that slot. In fact, critics of using the market to allocate slots have suggested that it is the *absence* of service to small markets that represents a failure of the competitive market that is, competitive markets for slots are likely to result in inefficient entry.[34]

On a practical level, it is nearly impossible for us to judge whether there is more surplus associated with a flight to destination A than a flight to destination B. For purposes of public policy, such a determination is required if either the hoarding or inefficient entry theories are applied to the regression results in Table 7.[35] An examination of Air Wisconsin's usage of its slots may illustrate this point. In all but 2 cases, Air Wisconsin used a four engine jet, a British Aerospace 146, listed as seating 112 passengers. This jet's design enables it to use short runways, meet Stage 3 noise requirements, and take-off and land at low cost, making it particularly suited for short-haul markets. Thus the negative and significant relationship between average daily capacity and slot share reported in Table 7 when United and Air Wisconsin are combined may represent the efficient use of a plane suited for use on short haul routes, and not anticompetitive behavior.

Alternatively, one can assume that United and Air Wisconsin are one airline, and that Air Wisconsin's usage of slots represent United's marginal slot usage. Under this assumption, Air Wisconsin flights using air carrier slots represent the leading carrier's marginal usage of slots during the weekdays. Table 8 lists the destinations served by Air Wisconsin flights using the slots contained in our dataset, as well as other carriers serving these destinations from Chicago. Examining Table 8 highlights the difficulty of carrying out policy based upon a carrier's route selection. In many cases, the service Air Wisconsin was providing

Table 8.   Air Wisconsin Destinations

City	Other Carriers With Direct Non-jet Service to Chicago	Other Carriers With Direct Jet Service to Chicago
AKRON, OH	AA, US*	AA
APPLETON, WI	—	—
CEDAR RAPIDS, IA	AA*	UA
CHAMPAIGN, IL	AA*, ML*	—**
CHARLESTON, WV	—	US
FORT WAYNE, IA	ML*	AA
GREEN BAY, WI	AA*, ML*	—
LEXINGTON, KY	US*	—
MILWAUKEE, WI	ML*	AA, ML, UA
MOLINE, IL	AA*, ML*	—
RICHMOND, VA	—	UA
ROANOKE, VA	—	—
TOLEDO, OH	AA*	—
WASHINGTON, DC	—	AA, ML, US, UA
WAUSAU, WI	AA*	—
YOUNGSTOWN, OH	—	—

Notes: AA = American Airlines
UA = United Airlines
US = USAir
ML = Midway (Service from Chicago Midway Airport).
Cities listed in **bold** are cities where Air Wisconsin offered the only jet service to Chicago.
  * Indicates service *via* code-sharing airline.
 ** Air Wisconsin used a turboprop (i.e., a non-jet Fokker 127) on this route. Thus the O'Hare-Champaign route had no jet service. On all other Air Wisconsin flights listed in this Table, a BA 146 jet was used.

was unique (e.g., the only service or the only direct jet service from an airport to Chicago). Of the 16 destinations listed in Table 8, three are not served by other direct service from Chicago, and at two of these three airports, Air Wisconsin provides the only service. To half of the 16 listed destinations, Air Wisconsin provided the only jet service. In 14 of the 16 cases, Air Wisconsin operated in direct competition with 2 or less airlines. In order to argue that the data implies Air Wisconsin's use of slots represents hoarding, one must argue that the surplus from flying to the destinations listed in Table 8 is less than the surplus that would be forthcoming if the slots were reallocated from United/Air Wisconsin. In addition, the data also is seemingly inconsistent with the inefficient entry hypothesis, that is, that the marginal slots will not be used to provide service in markets that could support only one or two firms.[36] Given this, it is unclear how a reallocation from United/Air Wisconsin would improve economic efficiency.

VI. CONCLUSION

In general, there is a positive and significant relationship between the rate at which a carrier uses a slot and the carrier's market share. Indeed, the two largest carriers at O'Hare, United and American, are among the most intensive users of slots. This is consistent with a theory of efficient use of slots by carriers owning a large share of the slots at a HDTA.

In addition, there is no evidence that the two largest carriers are using leasing as an anticompetitive device. Both American and United are net lessees of slots, and there is no significant difference between the rate of slot use of their owned and operated slots and their lessee's rate of slot use. The data also show that the two largest carriers, United and American, lease more slots for their own use than they lease for use by others. Both of these findings are inconsistent with the predictions of the anticompetitive leasing hypothesis.

In contrast, our results concerning capacity usage are consistent with both hoarding and efficiency hypotheses. Taken as a whole, however, the statistical evidence presented here does not imply that it is likely that concentration in the slot market at O'Hare was generating anticompetitive activity. Instead, the evidence is more consistent with the hypothesis that efficiency considerations were generating concentration at O'Hare.

ACKNOWLEDGMENTS

This paper was written while both authors were at the Federal Trade Commission. The views expressed in this paper are the authors', and do not necessarily reflect those of the Federal Trade Commission, nor those of any of its Commissioners. We are grateful to David Bennett, Scott Donnely, and Mark Castaldo at the FAA for providing us with the data.

We would like to thank Effie Stewart for research assistance on the project. The paper benefitted from helpful comments from Tim Daniel, Tim Dayek, John Lopatka, Paul Pautler, Mike Vita and participants at the Western Economic Association Conference, Southern Economic Association Conference, and in seminars at George Mason University School of Law, University of Toronto, and the Antitrust Division of the Department of Justice. Any errors are the responsibility of the authors.

NOTES

1. For example, while Coase (1960) explicitly suggested the use of market mechanisms to allocate the broadcast spectrum, current FCC restrictions on use and sale of spectrum nowhere approximates the regime described by Coase. For a public choice explanation of resistance to the use of markets in this area, see Hazlett (1990).

2. This is another area in which market oriented approaches have been applied in a limited form. See Hahn (1989).

3. For a detailed discussion of the events leading up to adoption of the market based slot transfer system, see Steed and Riker (1990).

4. See Grether, Isaac, and Plott (1981) and Department of Transportation, Federal Aviation Administration, High Density Traffic Airports; Slot Allocation and Transfer Methods, Final Rule; Request for Comments, 14 C.F.R. Parts 11 and 93, 50 Fed. Reg. 52180 (1985) (hereafter FAA 1985 Final Rule). Newark Airport was made an HDTA in 1968. Slot restrictions there, however, were soon eliminated and have not been reinstated, although Newark technically retains its HDTA status.

5. Incumbents, however, were allowed to trade slots with each other on a one for one basis. See FAA 1985 Final Rule, supra note 4, p. 52185.

6. For a detailed discussion of the effects of this six-week market, see Koran and Ogur (1983).

7. See FAA 1985 Final Rule, supra note 4, p. 52180, and 14 C.F.R. Parts 93.211-93.229.

8. See also 14 C.F.R. Part 93.215. Economists examining the problem of initially allocating slots advocated the use of auctions. See Grether, Isaac and Plott (1981). Steed and Riker (1990) suggest that use of grandfathering, which extended the transfer of wealth to the incumbent air carriers, was used to gain political support for the market-based system of transferring slots. Hazlett (1990) suggests similar considerations can be used to explain the rejection of the use of auctions to allocate the broadcast spectrum.

9. See 14 C.F.R. Part 93.227. The FAA clearly believes that carriers' property rights to use and sell slots are constrained, noting that "Slots do not

represent a property right but represent an operating privilege subject to absolute FAA control," see 14 C.F.R. Part 93.223.

10.   See U.S. General Accounting Office (1991). Borenstein (1989) found a similar 3-5 percent increase in yields at Chicago's O'Hare airport. His study focused on hubs, and therefore did not examine the other three HDTAs.

11.   See, for example, U.S. General Accounting Office (1990, pp. 21-30). See also Testimony and Exhibits of America West Airlines, Inc., DOT, USAir-Piedmont Acquisition case, Exhibit AWA T-1,2, Docket 44719, September 21, 1987. Some critics have also addressed distributional issues, observing that incumbent carriers received a valuable (and salable) right for free. See, for example, FAA 1985 Final Rule, supra note 4, p. 52184, and the discussion in note 8. Such distributional issues will not be addressed in this paper. While it might be better for the federal treasury that airlines pay for slots, the Coase (1960) Theorem implies that in the absence of transactions costs (which seem low), the initial allocation of rights does not affect the allocative efficiency of the final market allocation.

12.   See U.S. Department of Justice (1984). The Merger Guidelines use the Herfindahl-Hirschmann Index (HHI), which equals the sum of the squares of the market shares of all of the firms in the relevant market, to measure concentration. Under the DOJ Merger Guidelines approach, markets are "moderately concentrated" if their HHIs are between 1000 and 1800 and "highly concentrated" if their HHIs are greater than 1800.

13.   Concern about high concentration in slots at Washington National and LaGuardia was an important part of the ruling of a Department of Transportation administrative law judge in 1987 that would have prevented USAir from merging with Piedmont. See Recommended Decision of Administrative Law Judge Ronnie A. Yoder, USAir-Piedmont Acquisition Case, DOT Docket 44719, September 21, 1987, pp 90-102. This decision was later overturned by the Secretary of Transportation.

14.   For example, the apparent high concentration at O'Hare may be the result of its efficient use as a major hub by United and American. For a discussion of the efficiencies of hub networks, and non-monopoly based explanations of high concentration and price premia at hubs, see Kleit and Maynes (1992). See also, Morrison and Winston (1986) and Brueckner, Dyer, and Spiller (1992). For a general statement of this proposition, see, for example, Demsetz (1973).

15.   An illustration of how the HDTAs and their regional competitors could be considered to be in the same antitrust market is provided by positions taken by the DOJ in the Eastern Airlines bankruptcy proceedings. The DOJ opposed United's proposed purchase of Eastern's National Airport slots and facilities, on the grounds that it would "lessen competition" between Washington and other cities because United was already by far the largest carrier at Dulles International Airport and the acquisition would have also given it control of 20 percent of the slots at National. See ("Justice Deptartment to Dispute Deal for Eastern Slots," 1991) *Antitrust & Trade Regulation Report* 152 (January 31, 1991), 186

(February 7, 1991), and 272 (February 21, 1991). The DOJ, however, did not object to Northwest Airlines' purchase of those assets even though Northwest had more slots than United at National prior to the bankruptcy sale. Similarly, despite the fact that United was the largest carrier at O'Hare, the DOJ did not object to United's purchase of Eastern's O'Hare slots, a position consistent with considering Midway Airport flights to be in the same antitrust market as O'Hare flights.

16.   The fact that slots are scarce at one airport, and thus sell for positive prices, while landing rights are not scarce at another airport in the same region does not resolve whether the two airports are in the same antitrust market. Two regional airports can be in the same antitrust market even when prices for slots vary between the airports. However, an HDTA alone could be a relevant antitrust market, and anticompetitive price increases could occur, even when there is another non-slot constrained airport in the region that is a substitute at current prices. In antitrust law, the ambiguity of using price alone to determine antitrust markets when the market is already assumed to be monopolized is sometimes called the "cellophane trap" because of its association with the "cellophane" case, *U.S. v. E.I. du Pont de Nemours & Co.*, 351 U.S. 377, 404 (1956). The term refers to a failure to take into account whether an observed price is supracompetitive rather than competitive when determining whether certain products or services are in the same antitrust market.

17.   Leading antitrust scholars have suggested using changes in "physical" output to distinguish between procompetitive and anticompetitive practices. See Posner (1977) and Easterbrook (1984).

18.   This analysis assumes the number of slots allocated per hour is set so that full utilization of all the slots in a period would not induce large congestion effects. If congestion effects are induced by full utilization, a reduction in slot use may be efficient. That is, a dominant carrier may wish to purchase and not use a slot in order to reduce the costs associated with excess congestion and delays imposed on the large number of their flights operated in that slot period. Carriers with a small number of slots in that slot period would be affected less and would have a smaller incentive to internalize these costs.

19.   See Recommended Decision of Administrative Law Judge R. A. Yoder, USAir-Piedmont Acquisition Case, supra note 13, p. 93, and Testimony and Exhibits of America West, supra note 11, pp. 8-11. We note that this anticompetitive hypothesis may not be distinguishable from the situation where a potential entrant makes a false claim that it cannot obtain slots from private parties, pressed in order to gain them from the government for free. The current regulatory regime, which includes a slot market, cannot inhibit entry more than the previous regime of nontransferable historical allocations, in which entrants were unable to obtain slots under any circumstances. See Koran and Ogur (1983). For a similar argument, see Lott (1987).

20.   See, for example, GAO, supra note 11. In this scenario, airlines choose their competitors by leasing slots to them. In this way, the dominant firm(s) can

28   ANDREW N. KLEIT and BRUCE H. KOBAYASHI

ensure that less efficient firms will be competing with them for the same passengers, while simultaneously deterring the entry of more efficient firms. For a theoretical discussion of this effect, see, for example, Rockett (1990), which examines a single incumbent (with a patent) facing a limited number of potential entrants. Weakening either the single incumbent or limited entrant assumptions weakens this theoretical result. Thus, this theoretical result would be less likely to apply to airline markets where there is more than one incumbent or more than one equally efficient potential entrant. For a general discussion of the fragility of the entry deterrence models, see Malueg and Schwartz (1991), and Waldman (1991).

    21. Output tests that do not take into account all output choices by a hypothetical monopolist also can be ambiguous. When the unobserved and observed measures of quantity (e.g., days the slot was used and seats per plane) are highly complementary, a hypothetical monopolist may increase price, and both the observed and unobserved quantity above the efficient levels provided in a competitive market. See Leffler (1982).

    22. Of the 2,242 slots in the original dataset, 435 slots were restricted to commuter operations, 88 slots were restricted to international use, 7 were domestic slots being used with international flights, 4 were international slots operated domestically, and 220 slots were not allocated or otherwise restricted by the FAA.

    23. Because the FAA has proposed slot regulations based on all days (weekends included) and weekday only use, we report use statistics using both criteria. See, for example, FAA Supplemental Notice of Proposed Rulemaking, High Density Traffic Airports: Slot Allocation and Transfer Methods, 56 *Fed. Reg,* 46674 (September 13, 1991), p. 46677.

    24. The slot data and the figures reported in Table 2 include four slots, all held by American, that were listed as being used less than 65 percent of the time. Because no slots were withdrawn for nonuse during the May-June 1990 reporting period, these four slots may represent missing data rather than nonuse.

    25. See, FAA Final Rule, High Density Traffic Airports: Slot Allocation and Transfer Methods, 57 *Fed. Reg.* 37308 (August 18, 1992).

    26. Based on the data, United would have been nine operations short of complying at 4:45pm, and 26 operations short of complying at 5:15pm. American would have been nine operations short of complying at 4:15pm, and 21 operations short at 4:45pm. As noted in the text, all slots in these time periods could have been brought into compliance by shifting operations from adjacent time periods. This is possible because the number of operations in excess of the minimum required by the 80 percent rule in adjacent time periods (4:15pm and 5:45pm for United, 3:45pm and 5:15pm for American) exceeded any shortfall in the above mentioned periods.

    27. Earlier, the FAA also proposed a more stringent 90 percent rule based on weekday use only. See FAA Supplemental Notice of Proposed Rulemaking. Based on this more stringent rule and on the pattern of slot use contained in

the data, our review indicates that the proposed rule would only affect nine United slots and seven American slots. The number of affected slots could be reduced to 1 slot for United and 3 slots for American by shifting flights from adjacent slot periods.

28. The property right associated with a low numbered slot may be less clear than that associated with a high numbered slot because the low numbered slot is more likely to be withdrawn. If the absence of clearly defined property rights inhibits slot trading, low numbered slots would be less likely to move to their highest valued use. See Kleit (1991).

29. Because the dependent variable is censored at the maximum number of days in the period studied, OLS estimates of the slope coefficients are biased towards zero. To correct for this, the regressions for both all days and weekdays only were estimated using a Tobit procedure with an upper limit at the maximum number of days. Theoretically, a two limit tobit should have been run, with the lower limit set equal to the number of days corresponding to the 65% threshold of the FAA's use or lose rule. However, the bias from not specifying a lower limit is likely to be small given the small number of observations (three Northwest slots) at this lower threshold. See Greene (1981, pp. 505-513).

30. In cases where there was more than one slot holder, the slot was assigned, for purposes of calculating market shares, to the entity that held the slot the majority of the days during the two-month period.

31. The regressions reported in this paper do not include the four American slots that, according to the data, were used less than 65 percent of the time. Because no slots were withdrawn for failure to meet the FAA's "use or lose" standard during the period studied, these observations may represent missing data rather than nonuse. All of the regressions were also run with these observations (and their low usage rates) included; because no substantive changes arose, these regressions were not reported for expositional convenience.

32. The derivative of number of days operated with respect to slot share in the tobit regression equals $\Phi(z)(\sigma_1 + \alpha_4\text{LEASE} + \alpha_6\text{MULTIPLE OPERATOR} + \alpha_8\text{MULTIPLE HOLDER})$, where z is the product of the vector of coefficients (α') and a vector containing values of the independent variables (x), and $\Phi(z)$ is the value of the distribution function evaluated at z. The mean values of all variables were used to calculate the derivative reported. See Madalla (1983, pp. 159-160).

33. The critical slot share is given by $-\alpha_3/\alpha_4$. That is, if α_3 is negative and α_4 is positive, as they are in the weekdayonly regressions, the estimated coefficients imply that a slot leased from a carrier with a slot share greater than this ratio is likely to be used more intensively than the lessor uses its O&O slots. On the other hand, if α_3 is positive and α_4 is negative, as they are in the all days regressions, the estimated coefficients imply that a slot leased from a carrier with a slot share lower than this ratio will be used more intensively than the lessor uses its O&O slots.

34.   Thus, Borenstein (1988, p. 375) notes that "[I]n the absence of large differences in demand functions across markets, competitive market license allocation is likely to lead to too much entry in crowded markets and too little service in markets that could support only one or two firms." Such effects arise when there is not a high correlation between profitability and social surplus. Borenstein suggests two factors that give rise to such a divergence. First, he suggests that the "lumpy" nature of slots give rise to inframarginal output and noncapturable consumer surplus. He shows that under specific demand conditions, profits and social surplus will not be highly correlated across markets, leaving markets with higher social surplus unserved. Second, he suggests that much of the private profits from entry into markets with many *noncooperative* incumbents results from transfers from the incumbents, with little effect on social surplus. He argues that this "business stealing" effect may induce excessive entry into crowded markets, even though entry into uncrowded markets would result in greater social surplus.

35.   We note that similar attempts at regulations based on governments making such determinations, for example, FAA administered slot allocations and CAB route and fare regulation, have been universally condemned by economists. For a more complete discussion of the problems with CAB regulation, see, for example, Keeler (1972) and Douglas and Miller (1974).

36.   See the discussion in note 34.

REFERENCES

Alchian, A.A., & Allen, W.R. (1983). *Exchange and production: Competition, coordination, and control* (pp. 266-268). Belmont, CA: Wadsworth Publishing.

Borenstein, S.J. (1989). Hubs and high fares: Airport dominance and market power in the U.S. airline industry. *Rand Journal of Economics, 20*(3), 344-365.

Borenstein, S.J. (1988). On the efficiency of competitive markets for operating licenses. *Quarterly Journal of Economics, 103*(2), 357-386.

Brueckner, J.K., Dyer, N.J., & Spiller, P.T. (1992). Fare determination in airline hub-and-spoke Networks. *Rand Journal of Economics, 23*(3), 309-333.

Coase, R.A. (1960a). The Federal Communications Commission. *Journal of Law and Economics, 2*, 1-40.

Coase, R.A. (1960b). The problem of social cost. *Journal of Law and Economics, 3*, 1-44.

Demsetz, H. (1973). *The market concentration doctrine.* Washington, DC: American Enterprise Institute.

Douglas, G.W., & Miller III, J.C. (1974). *Economic regulation of domestic air transport: Theory and policy.* Washington, DC: Brookings.

Easterbrook, F.H. (1984). The limits of antitrust. *Texas Law Review, 63*(1), 1-40.

Greene, W.H. (1981). On the asymptotic bias of the ordinary least squares estimator of the tobit model. *Econometrica, 49*, 505-513.

Grether, D.M., Isaac, R.M, & Plott, C.R. (1981, May). The allocation of landing rights by unanimity among competitors. *American Economic Review, 71*, 166-171.

Hahn, R.W. (1989, Spring). Economic prescriptions for environmental problems: How the patient followed the doctor's orders. *Journal of Economic Perspectives, 3*(2), 95-114.

Hazlett, T. (1990). The rationality of U.S. regulation of the broadcast spectrum. *Journal of Law and Economics, 33*(1), 133-176.

Keeler, T.E. (1972). Airline regulation and market performance. *Bell Journal of Economics, 3*(2), 399-424.

"Justice Deptartment to dispute deal for eastern slots." (1991, February 15). *Washington Post*, pp. B2, 60

Kleit, A.N. (1991, Summer). Competition without apology: Market power and entry in the deregulated airline industry. *Regulation, 14*(3), 68-75.

Kleit, A.N., & Maynes, S.G. (1992). Airline networks as joint goods: Implications for market power analysis. *Journal of Regulatory Economics, 4*, 175-186.

Koran, D., & Ogur, J.D. (1983, May). *Airport access problems: Lessons learned from slot regulation by the FAA.* Washington, DC: Bureau of Economics Staff Report to the Federal Trade Commission.

Leffler, K.B. (1982). Ambiguous changes in product quality. *American Economic Review, 72*(5), 956-967.

Lott, Jr, J.R. (1987). Licensing and non-transferable rents. *American Economic Review, 77*(3), 453-455.

Madalla, G.S. (1983). *Limited dependent and qualitative variables in econometrics.* Cambridge, UK: Cambridge University Press.

Malueg, D., & Schwartz, M. (1991). Preemptive investment, toehold entry, and the mimicking principle. *Rand Journal of Economics, 22*(1), 1-13.

Morrison, S., & Winston, C. (1986). *The economic effects of airline deregulation.* Washington, DC: Brookings.

Posner, R.A. (1976). *Antitrust law: An economic perspective.* Chicago, IL: The University of Chicago Press.

Posner, R.A. (1977). The rule of reason and the economic Approach: Reflections on the *Sylvania* Decision. *The University of Chicago Law Review, 45*(1), 1-20.

Rockett, K.E. (1990, Spring). Choosing the competition and patent licensing. *Rand Journal of Economics, 21*(1), 161-171.

Steed, I., & Riker, W.H. (1990). *Common property and private property: The case of air slots* (mimeo.), University of Rochester.

U.S. Department of Justice. (1984, June 14). Merger guidelines. *Antitrust and Trade Regulation Report* No. 1169, Special Supplement.

U.S. General Accounting Office. (1990). *Airline competition: Industry operating and market practices limit entry.* GAO Report to Congressional Requesters, RCED 90-147.

U.S. General Accounting Office. (1991). *Airline competition: Effects of market concentration and barriers on airfares.* GAO Report to Congressional Requesters, RCED 91-101.

Waldman, M. (1991). The role of multiple potential entrants/sequential entry in noncooperative entry deterrence. *Rand Journal of Economics, 22*3, 446-453.

THE EFFECT OF
SOUTHWEST AIRLINES
ON U.S. AIRLINE MARKETS

Krista Richards

ABSTRACT

This paper estimates a series of fare equations to ascertain the effects of actual and potential competition by Southwest on markets for air travel. The results indicate that pricing strategies differ depending on Southwest's presence or potential presence on a route. Concentration is not found to be a determinant of airfares when a general specification is adopted. These results suggest that route characteristics other than just concentration need to be taken into account to evaluate the competitiveness of a route. In particular, the potential or actual presence of a low cost competitor seems to be a more important determinant of fares than conventional measures of concentration.

Research in Transportation Economics, Volume 4, pages 33-47.
Copyright © 1996 by JAI Press Inc.
All rights of reproduction in any form reserved.
ISBN: 1-55938-915-X.

33

I. INTRODUCTION

Since deregulation of the U.S. airline industry in 1978, there has been much debate as to what structure the industry would take. Over seventeen years later, the airline industry has not yet reached a long run equilibrium (Morrison & Winston, 1995). Prior to deregulation, nearly all economists agreed that deregulation of the airline industry would improve consumer welfare. Although most still do, the increase in concentration at the national level has prompted concerns as to the competitiveness of the industry.

A number of features have developed in the airline industry with the potential for increasing entry barriers, such as hub-and-spoke networks, computer reservation systems, frequent flyer programs, travel agent commission overrides, and slot restricted airports. Subsequently, many studies indicate that airline markets are not perfectly contestable (Joesch & Zick, 1994; Oum, Zhang, & Zhang, 1993; Whinston & Collins, 1992; Strassmann, 1990; Morrison & Winston, 1986).

Despite these findings, the experience of Southwest Airlines shows that it is possible to compete with hub-and-spoke systems by offering low-cost, no-frills, point-to-point service. Southwest was consistently profitable throughout the early 1990s, even though the industry as a whole experienced heavy losses. The low-cost, low-fare strategy of Southwest is having strong effects on the structure of the U.S. airline industry, leading some to believe that the long run equilibrium of the industry will include the Southwest model for short haul routes and hub-and-spoke systems for long haul routes (Morrison & Winston, 1995; Ellig & Winegarden, 1994).

The intent of this paper is to further investigate the effect of Southwest Airlines on markets for air travel.

II. BACKGROUND

Contestability theory was influential in the early predictions of industry structure. A contestable market is one in which entry and exit are entirely costless. Thus there would be potential for competitors to enter the market at any time. The theory maintains that the threat of potential competition is sufficient to induce firms to price at a competitive level (i.e., where price equals marginal costs) even in the absence of actual competition. It was argued that airline markets would be characterized by contestability because airline capital is virtually "capital on wings" and can thus enter and exit markets easily with little sunk costs (Baumol, Panzar, & Willig, 1988, p. 7).

If airline markets are contestable, then the level of market concentration would have no relationship to airfares since airfares would already be at their competitive level.[1] A number of studies investigate this and find a positive relationship between airfares and market concentration levels, suggesting that airline markets are not contestable (Joesch & Zick, 1994; Oum et al., 1993; Whinston & Collins, 1992; Strassmann, 1990; Morrison & Winston, 1986).

Some argue that airline markets were contestable in the period immediately following deregulation, but with the development of hub-and-spoke systems, frequent flyer programs, computer reservation systems, travel agent commission overrides, and slot constrained airports, there are now significant sunk costs involved in entering airline markets. Support for this idea comes from Joesch and Zick (1994) who find the relationship between market concentration[2] and airfares to be statistically insignificant in 1983, but positive and significant in 1987 and 1990.

Although there has been an increase in concentration at the national level, at the route level concentration has actually declined since deregulation (Leahy, 1994). Some argue that pricing power is conferred though airport dominance, not route concentration (Evans & Kessides, 1994, 1993; Borenstein, 1991; Morrison & Winston, 1990).

Another approach to this issue is to examine the ability of prices to signal potential entrants. Strassmann (1990) finds that future entry is influenced by current prices, whereas Joskow, Werden and Johnson (1994) find that entry is generally not induced by price levels substantially above the norm, instead both entry and exit occur most frequently on low-price city pairs. This is consistent with Morrison and Winston's (1990) findings that suggest that high fares may signal entry barriers or relatively high costs as opposed to supranormal profits. Nevertheless, entry has been observed to reduce fares and increase output (Joskow et al., 1990).

Although airline markets do not appear to be perfectly contestable, there is evidence to suggest that potential carriers do influence major carriers' actions (Morrison & Winston, 1986, p. 64; Lin, 1995). Furthermore, an exception to the findings of the noncontestability of airlines markets comes from Slovin, Sushka and Hudson (1991). They found that since deregulation, changes in concentration have no positive effect on carrier returns[3], supporting the idea of the contestability of airlines markets.

Although there is much evidence to suggest that dominance on a route signifies monopoly power which contributes to higher airfares, Southwest has demonstrated that this need not be the case. Even on routes where Southwest has a large market share, it offers lower fares than were previously offered by its competitors (Ellig & Winegarden, 1994). Ellig and Winegarden (1994) argue that it is because of Southwest's lower fares that they have earned high market shares. This is consistent with the findings of Oum and associates (1993) that the carrier using the more aggressive pricing strategy tends to secure a higher market share.

III. MODEL SPECIFICATION

To investigate the effect of Southwest Airlines on markets for air travel, a series of fare equations is estimated. Fare equations are estimated by many authors[4] to see how various aspects of competition affect fares. Such estimations usually involve regressing the fare or yield on a route on various cost variables, demand variables, and markup variables.

Lin (1995) estimated a model with intercept dummy variables used to capture the autonomous effects of Southwest's presense on yields. But such a specification may be too restrictive because the relationship between some of the explanatory variables, such as concentration, and airfares may also differ depending on whether Southwest is an actual or potential competitor on a route. Thus, to allow for a more general specification, three separate equations are estimated, one where Southwest serves the route (*SW*), another in which Southwest serves at least one of the endpoints of the route (*SWPOT*), and a control system of equations in which Southwest does not serve either endpoint of the routes in the sample (*NOSW*). A finding that there is no difference between the equations in which Southwest is an actual competitor, a potential competitor, or neither an actual nor potential competitor would lend support to the theory that airline markets are contestable.

For each of the three groups, the fare equation is estimated as part of a system of supply and demand. The model, derived from Joesch and Zick (1994) and Peteraf and Reed (1994), consists of a supply relation estimated in its inverse form with yield used as a proxy for price and a passenger demand equation. The yield or fare on a route is assumed to be a function of cost variables, passenger demand variables, and market structure variables. The number of passengers on a route is assumed to be a function of the fare on the route, the market size, and income. The structural model can be expressed as follows:

$$Y_i = f(C_i, P_i, M_i)$$

$$P_i = f(Y_i, I_i, R_i)$$

where Y_i is the average yield per passenger mile on route i, C_i is a vector of cost variables for route i, P_i is a vector of passenger demand variables for route i, M_i is a vector of market characteristic variables that affect pricing on route i, I_i is a variable to reflect the income level of the cities served by route i, and R_i is a vector of route characteristics variables that affect passenger demand on route i. The variables used in the estimation and their predicted effects follow.

Average length of haul is used as a measure of the cost of serving a route. Because of the fixed costs associated with takeoff, the length of haul is expected to have a negative relationship to yield per mile. The number of passengers is also expected to be negatively related to yield because higher load factors lead to declining unit-costs in serving additional passengers.

Table 1. Vacation Oriented Cities

Aspen, Colorado
Fort Lauderdale, Florida
Fort Myers, Florida
Hilo, Hawaii
Honolulu, Hawaii
Indio/Palm Springs, California
Jacksonville, Florida
Kahului, Hawaii
Kona, Hawaii
Las Vegas, Nevada
Lihue, Hawaii
Melbourne, Florida
New Orleans, Louisiana
Orlando, Florida
Reno, Nevada
Tampa, Florida
West Palm Beach, Florida

Several variables are utilized to determine the effects of various market characteristics on airfares. A Herfindahl-Hirschman Index (*HHI*) is calculated for each route included in the yield equation. If an increase in *HHI* leads to an increase in the average airfare, ceteris paribus, this is considered to be an indication that the market is not perfectly contestable.

A dummy variable is included to capture the effect on airfares that arises from one the endpoints being a major carrier's hub airport. Some studies have indicated that higher airfares are associated with hub airports (Evans & Kessides, 1994, 1993; Borenstein, 1991). This is to be expected if hub airports represent a barrier to entry. Likewise, slot-restricted airports have also been shown to have a positive relationship to airfares (Lin, 1995). Therefore, a dummy variable is included to control for this effect as well.

A vacation dummy variable is included to account for the lower proportion of business travelers on routes that are considered vacation oriented. The cities coded vacation oriented are listed in Table 1. It is expected that airfares will be lower on routes in which one of the endpoints is vacation oriented.

For the passenger demand equation, it is assumed that the number of passengers on a route is a function of the average yield, the income and population of the areas served by the route, and route characteristics, that is, whether the route is vacation oriented and whether substitute transportation modes were likely available for the route.

The system of equations is estimated using the two-stage-least-squares (2SLS) method. Yield and passengers are treated as endogenous and all of the exogenous variables are used as instruments. The model is specified in equations (1) and (2).

$$\ln(Y_i) = \alpha_{1j} + \alpha_{2j}\ln(AVHAUL_i) + \alpha_{3j}\ln(PASS_i) + \alpha_{4j}HHI_i$$
$$+ \alpha_{5j}VAC_i + \alpha_{6j}HUB_i + \alpha_{7j}SLOT_i + \epsilon_{1ij} \qquad (1)$$

$$\ln(PASS_i) = \beta_{1j} + \beta_{2j}\ln(Y_i) + \beta_{3j}\ln(POP_i) + \beta_{4j}\ln(INC_i)$$
$$+ \beta_{5j}SUB_i + \beta_{6j}VAC_i + \gamma_{2ij} \qquad (2)$$

where:

Y_i = average passenger revenue (in cents) per mile on route i

$AVHAUL_i$ = average miles traveled by a passenger on route i

$PASS_i$ = total number of passengers per day on route i

HHI_i = Herfindahl-Hirschman Index for route i

VAC_i = dummy variable equal to 1 if one of the endpoints of the route is vacation oriented, and 0 otherwise.

HUB_i = dummy variable equal to 1 if one of the endpoints is a hub of a major carrier, and 0 otherwise.

$SLOT_i$ = dummy variable equal to 1 if either one of the endpoints of route i is a city with a slot restricted airport, and 0 otherwise

POP_i = sum of the population of the two endpoints of route i

INC_i = sum of the total income of both endpoints of route i divided by the total population of both endpoints to give per capita income of route i

SUB_i = dummy variable to indicate the competition from substitute transportation modes, equal to 1 for routes less than 300 miles, and 0 otherwise

$i = 1,\ldots,I$ route observations

$j = 1,\ldots,J$ Southwest's presence-specific equations.

IV. DATA

The primary source of data is from the Department of Transportation's Origin-Destination (O-D) Survey of Airline Passenger Traffic for the top 1000 routes of the second quarter of 1995. The data in the O-D survey result from a continuous survey of ten percent of all the tickets sold in the United States. Because Southwest serves primarily short-haul routes, only routes of less than 1000 miles are used, resulting in a sample of 588 city-pair markets. Southwest serves 202 of the routes and is a potential competitor on 225 of the routes. The O-D survey includes data on average yields, length of haul, number of passengers, and on the market share of each carrier on a route. Information on Southwest's potential entry and the Herfindahl-Hirschman Index are derived from this data.

Table 2.   Descriptive Statistics
Pooled Sample
($N = 588$)

Variable	Mean	Standard Deviation
Y	23.463	13.448
AVHAUL	581.804	257.269
PASS	390.662	483.580
HHI	.556	.199
POP	5195.75	2838.26
INC	22136.68	2372.12
SUB	.172	.378
VAC	.245	.430
HUB	.757	.429
SLOT	.202	.402

Table 3. Descriptive Statistics
SW Sample
(N = 203)

Variable	Mean	Standard Deviation
Y	15.459	5.860
AVHAUL	522.714	226.958
PASS	479.513	465.211
HHI	.535	.187
POP	4598.57	2777.21
INC	20991.47	2136.16
SUB	.192	.395
VAC	.187	.391
HUB	.621	.486
SLOT	.084	.278

Table 4. Descriptive Statistics
SWPOT Sample
(N = 225)

Variable	Mean	Standard Deviation
Y	25.677	12.64
AVHAUL	657.64	244.706
PASS	313.585	402.299
HHI	.571	.202
POP	5426.54	2800.20
INC	22491.18	1934.09
SUB	.076	.265
VAC	.204	.404
HUB	.827	.379
SLOT	.204	.404

Income and population data were collected from Local Area Personal Income 1969-1992 (U.S. Department of Commerce). Metropolitan area data are used for most cities. County area data are used for smaller cities in which metropolitan area data are not available. Information on income and population in Puerto Rico, the Virgin Islands, and Guam is not available from this source, therefore the model is estimated without those observations with endpoints in the aforementioned locales. Income and population data from 1992 are the most recent available and are thus used as a proxy for 1995 income and population data.

Table 5. Descriptive Statistics
NOSW Sample
(N = 160)

Variable	Mean	Standard Deviation
Y	30.506	16.133
AVHAUL	550.125	284.507
PASS	386.323	584.697
HHI	.561	.209
POP	5628.88	2859.27
INC	23091.13	2633.92
SUB	.281	.451
VAC	.375	.487
HUB	.831	.376
SLOT	.350	.478

Descriptive statistics of the variables used in the estimations are shown in Tables 1-4. The mean average yield per mile is 15.459, 25.6787, and 31.288 for the SW, $SWPOT$, and $NOSW$ samples respectively, which equates to one-way average fares of \$80.81, \$168.86, and \$168.56.

V. RESULTS

The results of the regressions are shown in Table 6. Most of the coefficients have the expected sign, with the exception of the $LNPASS$ coefficient in the pooled equation. The coefficients on $LNPASS$ in the SW, $SWPOT$, and $NOSW$ equations are negative, as expected, but are not significant. The coefficient on $LNAVHAUL$ is negative and significant in all of the equations indicating that yields per mile fall as the length of haul increases. The vacation dummy variable has a negative and significant effect on yields in all of the equations implying that vacation oriented routes tend to have lower airfares, all else constant. Hub airports are shown to have a positive and significant effect on yields in all of the equations estimated. The coefficient on HHI is positive and significant in the pooled equation, yet is not significant in the other equations, implying that concentration has a positive effect on

Table 6. 2SLS Coefficient Estimates
(Dependent Variable $=$ *LNY*)

Variable	Pooled	SW	SWPOT	NOSW
INTERCEPT	3.856**	6.230**	5.727**	9.608**
	(.908)	(.486)	(.825)	(2.745)
LNAVHAUL	-.391**	-.544**	-.416**	-.651**
	(.053)	(.046)	(.063)	(.084)
LNPASS	.182***	-.038	-.049	-.419
	(.106)	(.037)	(.130)	(.374)
HHI	.644**	-.043	.187	-.212
	(.142)	(.091)	(.159)	(.560)
VAC	-.093*	-.089**	-.259**	-.387**
	(.048)	(.036)	(.079)	(.077)
HUB	.288**	.079**	.290**	.221*
	(.048)	(.031)	(.073)	(.097)
SLOT	.229**	.171**	.190*	.121
	(.060)	(.058)	(.095)	(.104)
Adjusted R^2	.34	.61	.36	.55

Notes: *SW* = sample in which Southwest serves the route.
SWPOT = sample in which Southwest serves at least one of the endpoints of the route.
NOSW = sample in which Southwest does not serve either endpoint of the route.
Standard errors are in parentheses.
** Indicates significance at the 1 percent level.
* Indicates significance at the 5 percent level.
*** Indicates significance at the 10 percent level.

airfares only when these other route characteristics are not taken into account.

An *F*-statistic[5] is calculated to test the hypothesis that the parameters in the *SW*, *SWPOT*, and *NOSW* equations are equivalent to the parameters in the pooled equation, that is, H_0: *apooled* $=$ *aSW* $=$ *aSWPOT* $=$ *aNOSW*, for each of the parameters, where "*a*" denotes the estimated value of α. The hypothesis is rejected at the 1 percent level.

A series of *t*-tests on individual coefficients are then performed to ascertain the differences between the equations. Specifically, the following hypotheses are tested for each of the parameters: H_1: *aSW* $=$ *aSWPOT*; H_2: *aSW* $=$ *aNOSW*; H_3: *aSWPOT* $=$ *aNOSW*.

The intercept in the *SW* equation and the intercept in the *SWPOT* equation are significantly lower than the intercept in the *NOSW* equation indicating that actual or potential competition by Southwest has a negative impact on yields, all else constant. The intercepts in the *SW* and *SWPOT* equations are not significantly different than one another.

There are some differences in the effect of average haul on yields between the three equations. This may be due to the differences in costs faced by different carriers or it may reflect differences in the costs of serving different routes.

Vacation oriented routes have a significantly greater (negative) effect on yields for the *SWPOT* and *NOSW* equations than for the *SW* equation. Likewise, the coefficients on *HUB* are significantly greater in the *SWPOT* and *NOSW* equations than in the *SW* equation. This may be because Southwest offers consistently low fares overall such that the differential between fares on vacation oriented and non-vacation oriented routes (or between fares on routes that involve a hub airport and routes that do not) would be less on routes in which Southwest is a competitor.

Slot restricted airports have a positive effect on yields in all of the equations and the effect is not significantly different between the three equations.

VI. CONCLUSION

This paper involved the estimation of a series of equations in order to ascertain the effects of actual and potential competition by Southwest on markets for air travel. The results indicate that pricing strategies differ depending on whether Southwest is an actual competitor, a potential competitor, or not a competitor at all on the route. Although some of the differences appeared to be due to differences in costs, the differences in the effects of the market characteristic variables on yields suggest that the pricing strategy on a route depends in part on the actual or potential carrier that is present on the route. This is not consistent with contestability theory which assumes that prices are a function of sunk costs.

The differences between the equations indicate that the more general specification is preferred to the restricted specification using the pooled sample. The finding that concentration does not have a significant impact on yields when a more general specification is adopted suggests that the positive relationship between concentration and yields found in previous studies may have been spurious. Although such a finding would tend to support the theory that airline markets are contestable, the differences that exist between the markets in which Southwest is an actual or potential competitor clearly do not support such a theory.

The implication of these results is that high concentration by itself is not an indicator that a route is not competitive. Other route characteristics, such as whether a low cost carrier serves the route, need to be taken into account to evaluate the competitiveness of a route.

ACKNOWLEDGMENT

I would like to express my appreciation to those who assisted with this research project. First, a special note of gratitude is extended to Starr McMullen for obtaining the data necessary for the project as well as providing guidance and support. My appreciation is also extended to Victor Tremblay and Laura Connolly for the useful comments they provided as well as the time the devoted on behalf of this project. I would also like to thank Transportation Northwest for enabling me to usc the computer facilities at the University of Washington.

NOTES

1. It is acknowledged that there could be other reasons why an airline may choose to price competitively, such as a Bertrand pricing strategy.

2. Measured at the route level.

3. This result may be due to the different methodology used by Slovin and associates (1991). They looked at the changes in excess returns around airline acquisition announcements to test whether excess returns are functions of concentration or hub dominance.

4. See Evans and Kessides (1993); Joesch and Zick (1994); Peteraf and Reed (1994); Lin (1995); Morrison and Winston (1995).

5. $F(21,560) = 36.86$.

REFERENCES

Baumol, W.J., Panzar, J.C., & Willig, R.D. (1988). *Contestable markets and the theory of industry structure* (Rev. ed.). San Diego, CA: Harcourt Brace Jovanovich.

Borenstein, S. (1990). Airline mergers, airport dominance, and market power. *American Economic Review, 80*(2), 400-404.

Borenstein, S. (1991). The dominant-firm advantage in multiproduct industries: Evidence from the U.S. airlines. *The Quarterly Journal of Economics, 106*(4), 1237-1266.

Borenstein, S. (1992). The evolution of U.S. airline competition. *Journal of Economic Perspectives, 6*(2), 45-73.

Ellig, J., & Winegarden, W.H. (1994). Airline policy and consumer welfare. *Transportation Practitioners Journal, 61*(4), 411-431.

Evans, W.N., & Kessides, I.N. (1993). Localized market power in the U.S. airline industry. *Review of Economics and Statistics, 75*(1), 66-75.

Evans, W.N., & Kessides, I.N. (1994). Living by the 'Golden Rule': Multimarket contact in the U.S. airline industry. *Quarterly Journal of Economics, 109*(2), 341-366.

Joesch, J.M., & Zick, C.D. (1994). Evidence of changing contestability in commercial airline markets during the 1980s. *Journal of Consumer Affairs, 28*(1), 1-24.

Joskow, A.S., Werden, G.J., & Johnson, R.J. (1994). Entry, exit, and performance in airline markets. *International Journal Of Industrial Organization, 12*(4), 457-471.

Leahy, A.S. (1994). Concentration in the U.S. airline industry. *International Journal of Transport Economics, 21*(2), 209-215.

Lin, J-S. (1995). *Concentration, entry, and potential entry: The impact of Southwest Airlines on the U.S. airline industry.* Transportation Research Forum Student Paper Contest.

Morrison, S.A., & Winston, C. (1986). *The economic effects of airline deregulation.* Washington DC: Brookings Institution.

Morrison, S.A., & Winston, C. (1990). The dynamics of airline pricing and competition. *American Economic Review, 80*(2), 389-393.

Morrison, S.A., & Winston, C. (1995). *The evolution of the airline industry.* Washington DC: Brookings Institution.

Oum, T.H., Zhang A., & Zhang, Y. (1993). Inter-firm rivalry and firm-specific price elasticities in deregulated airline markets. *Journal of Transport Economics and Policy, 27*(2), 171-192.

Peteraf, M.A., & Reed, R. (1994, April). Pricing and performance in monopoly airline markets. *Journal of Law and Economics, 37*, 193-213.

Slovin, M.B., Sushka, M.E., & Hudson, C.D. (1991). Deregulation, contestability, and airline acquisitions. *Journal of Financial Economics, 30*(2), 231-251.

Strassmann, D.L. (1990). Potential competition in the deregulated airlines. *Review of Economics and Statistics, 72*(4), 696-702.

U.S. Department of Commerce. (1994). *Local Area Personal Income 1969-1992.* Washington DC: Economics and Statistics Administration, Bureau of Economics.

Whinston, M.D., & Collins, S.C. (1992). Entry and competitive structure in deregulated airline markets: An event study analysis of people express. *RAND Journal of Economics, 23*(4), 445-462.

LEGISLATED MARKET DOMINANCE
IN RAILROAD MARKETS

Wesley W. Wilson

ABSTRACT

Under current regulatory rules in the railroad industry, railroad
rates are not subject to reasonableness proceedings unless the
Surface Transportation Board of the Department of Transportation finds that the railroad is "market dominant." A theoretical
model of railroad pricing is used here to examine and interpret the
regulatory rules defining market dominance. Railroad rates in a
market are either market dominant, constrained market dominant,
or not market dominant. The empirical analysis evaluates the
effects of competitive pressures on rates. Competition is found to
reduce grain rates by up to 40 percent and service differentials
across competing modes explain only a portion of observed rate
levels.

Research in Transportation Economics, Volume 4, pages 49-67.
Copyright © 1996 by JAI Press Inc.
All rights of reproduction in any form reserved.
ISBN: 1-55938-915-X.

I. INTRODUCTION

Recent legislation affecting transportation industries has tended toward placing greater reliance on the marketplace to establish prices and less reliance on the regulatory authority. In the railroad industry, the Staggers Rail Act of 1980 amended transport policy "...to allow, to the maximum extent possible, competition and the demand for services to establish rates for transportation by rail."[1] Under this policy, a rate set by a railroad is not subject to rate regulation unless the Surface Transportation Board of the Department of Transportation finds the railroad to be market dominant. If the railroad is found to be market dominant, then and only then may the reasonableness of the rate be considered. Consequently, market dominance is essentially a screening mechanism in the regulatory process by which potentially reasonable and unreasonable rates are delineated (Tye, 1984a).

Market dominance, as defined by the Railroad Revitalization and Regulatory Reform Act of 1976 (the 4-R Act), the Staggers Rail Act of 1980, and subsequent Interstate Commerce Commission proceedings, involves a qualitative evaluation of competitive pressures (e.g., intramodal, intermodal, product, and geographic competition).[2] As such, legislative interpretation of the concept of market dominance is somewhat normative and a matter of debate in regulatory practice and theoretical analyses.[3] Essentially, the arguments posed by proponents suggest that because of receiver and/or supplier alternatives, the forces of intramodal, intermodal, product, and/or geographic competition force the railroad to price competitively because the railroad can ill afford to price its shippers out of the market. Adversaries point out that a mere demonstration that the railroad in question is not a monopolist does not necessarily imply that competition is an effective constraint on pricing. Reconciliation of these two views is an important contribution of this paper.

This issue of market dominance, of course, was central in the Cellophane Case.[4] As discussed in Froeb and Werden (1992) the Supreme Court found that "because there were many reasonably good substitutes for its product" du Pont did not violate Section 2 of the Sherman Act. A difficulty of such a criterion in establishing market dominance is that such competitors may exist because of market dominance—the competitors may exist because the firm exerts market power leading to prices high enough to support inefficient competitors. The model presented in this paper defines market dominance not only in terms of the presence of competitor or competing alternatives but also in terms of the effectiveness of those competitors. The result allows the two views that alternatives are competitive forces and alternatives may not be effective, to be reconciled.

Market dominance is examined here in the context of railroad pricing. Section II provides a review of the history of market dominance standards in railroad regulation. In Section III, market dominance standards that have evolved in the regulatory environment are integrated into a disaggregate model of railroad pricing.[5] Demanders (shippers) are modeled as making discrete decisions pertaining to products shipped, shipment locations, and mode choice. By modeling these decisions, the forces of market dominance, product, geographic, intramodal and intermodal competition, are represented. The result provides a theoretical measure of market dominance that can be directly linked to legislated market dominance.

It has been argued that the usual market dominant standards are implicit in railroad pricing insofar as such concepts are implied by the transportation demand elasticity confronting the railroad.[6] That result is a special case of this model. In particular, the model of railroad pricing, reflecting modal, geographic, and product competition, suggests rates may be the result of one of three cases. These include: (1) competitive pressures are not effective and the railroad is the "dominant" mode; (2) competitive pressures are "effective" and restrict railroad pricing decisions; and (3) competitive pressures are effective but the railroad is not the dominant mode. The model is illustrated with evidence presented in the McCarty Farms case.[7] In this case, where the ICC found the railroad market-dominant, the model developed here finds rates that are up to 40 percent higher than rates in comparable markets where the railroad is not "strictly" market-dominant.

II. MARKET DOMINANCE AND REGULATION

Historically, the ICC has had broad jurisdictional powers over determination of interstate rail rates. Prior to passage of the 4-R Act, the ICC had jurisdiction over all interstate railroad rates, using a "just and reasonable" standard.[8] Beginning with the 4-R Act and culminating with the Stagger's Rail Act of 1980, transportation policy shifted focus to the ability of the marketplace to regulate prices. For example, the Stagger's Rail Act amended transportation policy "...to allow, to the maximum extent possible, competition and the demand for rail services to establish rates for transportation by rail."

Passage of the 4-R Act introduced the concept of market dominance into the regulatory environment.[9] As defined by the 4-R Act, market dominance pertained to "an absence of effective competition from other carriers or modes of transportation for the traffic or movement to which a rate applies." The ICC subsequently established guidelines for market dominance.[10] These guidelines included criteria that would give the ICC jurisdiction to consider the reasonableness of the rate under question. These criteria included a market-share measure (whether the railroad had over 70 percent of the traffic) and a performance measure (whether the rate relative to variable cost was over 160 percent).[11]

In principle, the market share-criterion introduces both intramodal and intermodal competition explicitly into the regulatory framework. The performance criterion, on the other hand, provides an explicit measure of the effectiveness of existing competition. For homogeneous products, these measures imply a formal linkage between the Lerner Index (percentage markup of price over marginal cost) and market shares (Raab, 1980; Saving, 1978).[12]

Prior to passage of the Staggers Rail Act of 1980, the market dominance criteria were rebuttable. If market dominance was established the ICC would have jurisdiction over the rate. On the other hand, if the market dominance criteria were not satisfied, the shipper(s) could rebut the finding of no market dominance. In regulatory practice, under these rules, Friedlaender and Spady (1981) noted that "The commission has interpreted the existence of 'market dominance' in a narrow fashion…and generally prevented rate increases in the case where only one railroad serves a given area, even though trucks may offer substantial competitive alternatives."

Passage of the Staggers Rail Act of 1980 fundamentally changed market dominance standards in two ways. First, the performance standard (revenue to variable cost) thresholds were established through time and were made non-rebuttable if satisfied. That is, if the revenue to variable cost ratio was below the current threshold, the rate was immune from ICC jurisdiction (i.e., the railroad is not market dominant).[13] Second, the Act introduced product competition to be considered in determination of rate reasonableness. In light of these changes, the ICC subsequently replaced its earlier market dominance rules with a qualitative evaluation of product, geographic, intramodal, and intermodal competition.[14] Product competition was interpreted essentially as the economic capability of a shipper (supplier or receiver) to use an alternative or substitute product rather than the product transported. Geographic competition pertained to the capability of a receiver or supplier to originate the product from another source, or to ship it to another destination.

As discussed in Eaton and Center (1985), these concepts have been widely employed and are founded in antitrust litigation. They note that the fundamental criterion for product competition is the cross-elasticity of demand and/or supply between the product and its substitute. On the other hand, interpretation of geographic competition is based on the area beyond which the company can sell its product. The salient aspect of geographic competition in transportation markets then becomes one of determining the areas from which a shipper or receiver can obtain the product from, based on delivered prices.

III.   MARKET DOMINANCE AND PRICING

Currently, "market dominance" is a qualitative finding, based on modal, product, and geographic competitive pressures. Little research has been conducted linking theory and regulatory practice. The model develop in this section allows formal interpretation of legislated market dominance. Central to the model of pricing is the behavior of demand, which has received considerable attention in the transportation literature. Winston (1981, 1983, 1985) delineates these studies into two dimensions: aggregate and disaggregate. In aggregate studies, multiple shipments over some time horizon are analyzed (Oum, 1979; Friedlaender & Spady, 1980; Boyer, 1977; Levin, 1978). In disaggregate studies, decisions pertaining to mode, quantity, and/ or geographic market for a single shipment are examined at a given point in time (Winston, 1981; Daughety & Inaba, 1977; McFadden, Winston, & Boersch-Supan, 1985; Inaba & Wallace, 1989). Some researchers maintain that the disaggregate approach to modeling demand is the preferred approach. For example, Winston suggests that the disaggregate approach is more firmly grounded in the institutional realities of decision making, allows a "richer" empirical specification, and allows a better understanding of competitive elements.[15] As demonstrated in this section, the disaggregate approach provides a methodology to examine the impact of competitive pressures on railroad prices in a disaggregate setting and develops a measurable index for market dominance.[16]

Consider the necessary conditions for a specific trade to take place between a given buyer and seller. In a price discovery framework, either the buyer or the seller of a product quotes the "terms of trade" regarding price, quantity, delivery, and so forth. The trade takes place only if the offer received dominates all other offers. Transportation costs enter into terms of the offer and into the decision to accept the offer.

A railroad must compete with other modes to obtain the traffic (modal competition). In addition, the railroad operating in a given market must also compete with markets defined as other origins and destinations (geographic competition), or substitute products (product competition). The importance of such constraints on railroad pricing was demonstrated by Dempsey, who stated, "...The constraint is the fact a railroad is in business to move traffic. It has no interest in pushing the rate to a level that would force its own shipper out of the market."[17] Thus, to be in a market, a railroad must choose a price that it is the preferred choice, given other modes and other geographic and product options. Of course, the railroad may choose not to be in the market that is, there is traffic that the railroad does not seek (e.g., unprofitable branch lines). Each of these choices is embedded in the following model.

At the disaggregate level, the firm demanding transportation chooses not only the quantity to be shipped but also the mode by which the product is shipped. In the case of receivers, the particular product shipped and the origination of the product are also choice variables. In the case of suppliers, the terminal market (i.e., destination) is also chosen.[18] With the exception of the quantities, the choice variables are discrete, consisting of the mode, the origination, the terminal market, and the product shipped.[19] These choices may or may not be options depending on whether a receiver or a supplier is the decision maker.[20] In either case, the railroad's problem is to choose a price that maximizes profit.

Generally, transport demand decisions are reflected in the associated production technology $T(Q,X)$, where Q is a vector of outputs and X is a vector of inputs. In recognition of the discrete nature of transportation decisions, the transformation function is a set of discrete alternatives represented by

$$T(Q,X) = \{T_1(Q_1, X_1), \ldots, T_N(Q_N, X_N)\} \qquad (1)$$

where: $T_i(Q_i, X_i)$ represents the ith technology; Q_i represents the output vector under the ith subtechnology; and X_i represents the input vector under the ith technology. In this framework, the firm demanding transport compares each potential subtechnology and chooses the particular subtechnology and input/output combinations yielding maximum profit. For example, a grain elevator operator simultaneously chooses the amount of grain to ship, the destination, and the mode.

Given price-taking demanders that engage in profit-maximizing behavior, and assuming the technology satisfies the appropriate regularity conditions,[21] there exists a set of profit functions describing maximal profits for each subtechnology. This set is

$$\pi = \{\pi_1(P,W), \ldots, \pi_N(P,W)\} \qquad (2)$$

where: π_i is the profit function associated with the ith subtechnology; P is the vector of output prices; and W is the vector of input prices.

The firm chooses the particular subtechnology (i.e., mode, source, terminal, or product as appropriate) which yield the maximum profit level. The choice i at given prices must satisfy $\pi_i(P,W) \geq \pi_j(P,W)$ for all j. Using Hotelling's lemma, the demand function facing the railroad is

$$-\partial \pi_i / \partial W_i = X_i^*(P, W) \text{ for } \pi_i \geq \pi_j \qquad (3)$$

All other potential inputs pertaining to alternative discrete options are not chosen and set equal to zero for $j \neq i$. In such a case, demand for transportation depends critically on the differences in the opportunity set or technology. When confronted with a change in rail rates, the subtechnology choice as well as the quantity choice are reevaluated.

A railroad's pricing decision is limited by the constraint that a substitute (competitive) technology (i.e., either a substitute factor of production, the same or different factor from another source, an alternative mode, or an alternative terminal) is not chosen by the demander. The model is also general in the sense that the resulting price may be restricted by the threat of entry by a nonexistent competitor (e.g., the price may be constrained by the stand-alone costs of a potential entrant) or alternative. This model then reflects the profit-maximizing notion that the railroad will not charge a price so high as to price itself out of the market. However, firms will charge a price as near to the monopoly price as possible. The profit-maximization problem is given by

$$MAX_{W_i} \pi^R = W_i X_i^*(W_i) - C(X_i^*(W_i)) \text{ s.t. } \pi_i \geq \pi_j \text{ for all } j. \qquad (4)$$

Where W_i is taken as the rail rate. The Lagrangian is given by

$$L = W_i X_i^*(W_i) - C(X_i^*(W_i)) + \lambda \{\pi_i - \pi_j\} \qquad (5)$$

and the associated first order conditions by

$$\partial L / \partial W_i = \{W_i - MC_i\}\partial X_i / \partial W_i + X_i(W_i) + \lambda \partial \pi_i / \partial W_i \leq 0 \quad (6)$$

$$\partial L / \partial \lambda = \pi_i - \pi_j \geq 0. \quad (7)$$

Again, by Hotelling's lemma, $\partial \pi / \partial W_i = -X_i$, allowing equation (6) to be rewritten

$$(W_i - MC_i) / W_i = (\lambda - 1) / \epsilon \quad (8)$$

where ϵ is the price elasticity of demand.

The left-hand side of equation (8) is the Lerner index of market performance. In this model, performance depends on the price elasticity of demand (ϵ) and the restrictiveness of competitive pressures (λ). The restrictiveness of competitive pressures is measured by the Lagrangian multiplier on the constraint that the railroad is the preferred choice and that the shipment made is preferred to other alternatives. This multiplier, λ, must lie in the closed interval [0,1]. At values greater than one, the railroad is the high cost producer and cannot compete even at marginal cost with the other discrete options (i.e., substitute subtechnologies) of the demanding firms. This case pertains to prices where the constrained price (W^*) is less than W the competitive ideal (W^c), that is, $W^* < W^c$). In such a case, the railroad cannot be considered market dominant. At values less than zero, the railroad is not profit-maximizing and can increase profit by reducing its price (i.e., $W^* > W^M$). Values of λ at the extremes, zero and one, reflect the standard monopoly (W^M) and competitive outcomes (W^c).

The concept of market dominance can be interpreted directly from these results. When the railroad is the low-cost alternative, at least the possibility for market dominance exists. However, market dominance cannot be considered a discrete finding except in the case where $W^* \geq W^m$. That is, when the railroad is the low-cost producer, it is considered strictly market dominant only when the monopoly price is obtained. Of course, a monopoly is, by definition, market dominant in the sense that at the monopoly price the railroad faces no actual or potential competition.

In the intermediate range, $W^c < W^* < W^M$, market dominance is a matter of degree. Competitive pressures constrain the market power of the railroad such that the observed price lies between the monopoly price and the competitive price. The range of prices over which competitive pressures may be effective depends on the price elasticity of demand for transport. When demand is relatively elastic, the range of rail prices is quite small. On the other hand, when demand is relatively more inelastic, the possible range of prices is larger.

In evaluating the effectiveness of competitive pressures in restricting rail rates, the model points to a number of important considerations. The critical variable in evaluating the effectiveness of product, geographic, modal, and/or "hit and run" entry by a stand-alone competitor, is the rail rate which causes the shipper/receiver to use a different product (e.g., a substitute input), to ship to or receive from a different location, or to use an alternative mode. Since differing discrete alternatives have different attributes, direct comparisons of rates and/or cost of providing the services are only relevant in defining the rail rate necessary to induce demanders to switch to another discrete alternative.

IV.   ILLUSTRATION—McCARTY FARMS

The implications and uses of the model are illustrated using the McCarty Farms Case (ICC Docket No. 37809).[22] This case pertains to the movement of wheat and barley from Montana to the Pacific Northwest. In 1980, Montana grain farmers initiated proceedings against the Burlington Northern (BN) charging unreasonable transportation charges and seeking reparations. In 1981, an ICC Administrative Law judge found that the BN had market dominance and rates were unreasonable insofar as they exceeded two hundred percent of the variable cost of service. The case was decided in favor of the complainant—The Burlington Northern was found to be market dominant and rates unreasonable. Throughout the case, a primary focus was the issue of market dominance. Evidence from this case, including intramodal, intermodal, product, and geographic dimensions, is used here to analyze the theory and regulatory practice of market dominance. In particular, evidence is used to evaluate rate savings from having competitive pressures present.

Implicit in this analysis is the assumption that the variable cost measurement used in these proceedings was a reasonable approximation of marginal cost.[23] Given this assumption, the percent markdown from the monopoly price can be calculated. First, equation (8) is written in terms of the revenue/marginal cost ratio:

$$\frac{W}{MC} = \frac{1}{1 - (\lambda - 1)/\epsilon} \qquad (9)$$

The performance standards reported for the movement of Montana wheat and barley to the PNW were revenue-to-variable cost ratios of 240 and 250 percent, while from all other origins these ratios were 186 to 156 percent, respectively (Montana State Department of Commerce). If the BN was market dominant in the sense that the 240 and 250 percent figures represent monopoly solutions, this implies elasticities of transport demand of -1.714 and -1.66, respectively. The corresponding implied elasticities for other regions are -2.163 and -2.7857 (if $\lambda = 0$). If the structural elasticity of demand at the monopoly point is the Montana solution, while the corresponding elasticity of demand represented by other regions is the constrained solution,[24] the implied values for λ are 20.75 percent for wheat and 40.41 percent for barley.[25] That is, in areas outside of Montana, competitive pressures mark the monopoly price downward by 20.75 and 40.41 percent for wheat and barley, respectively.

The estimates of the markdown from the monopoly price measured by λ may be reflective of a variety of different factors. The evidence submitted suggests that railroads are generally the "low cost" mode. However, different modes have different service attributes. The value demanders place on such attributes is critical to the decision of which mode to use. The model allows an estimate of the value of these service attributes.

Assume the railroad prices up to the constraint that the demander is indifferent between modes of transportation. In equilibrium, the price of the competing mode (taken as

competitive) is written as a markup or a markdown of the rail price
as follows:

$$t = rs \qquad (10)$$

where: t is the price associated with the other mode;
r is the price associated with the rail mode; and
s is the premium markup ($s > 1$) or discount ($s < 1$) factor
associated with the alternative mode relative to the rail
mode.

Short-run equilibrium in the alternative mode market requires

$$t = MC_t \qquad (11)$$

where MC_t is the marginal cost of the competitive mode. Observed
in the evidence is the percentage markup of the rail rate to variable
costs (k) and the relationship of alternative mode (truck $-$ barge)
costs to rail costs.

$$(r - MC_r)/r = k \qquad (12)$$

Substitution of (10) into (11) for t and the result in (12) yields (13)
after rearrangement.

$$s = (1-k)MC_t/MC_r \qquad (13)$$

In (13), s is interpreted directly as a markup (markdown) factor
associated with values placed on differing service attributes. In
effect, the larger is s, the larger is the value placed on alternative-
mode attributes relative to the rail mode. Hence, even though the
railroad is the low-cost mode (i.e., on a marginal cost basis), the
rate charged is constrained by the implicit premiums placed on
service attributes.

When $s = 1$, relative service attributes are valued the same. In
this case, the railroad price is constrained simply to the difference
in costs between the two modes. Specifically, if prices are the same,
the other alternative is priced at marginal cost. The larger is the

Table 1. Service Premium Factors (derived *s* values)

Cost Factor	Barley (k = .6)	Wheat (k = .58)
1.61	0.64	0.67
1.85	0.74	0.77

value placed on service attributes on the alternative mode relative to the rail mode ($s > 1$) the smaller is the departure of the rail price from the other mode's cost. On the other hand, when the railroad has preferred service attributes ($s > 1$), the greater is the departure from the other modes cost—rail pricing power is enhanced.

In the evidence, MC_t/MC_r ranges from 1.61 to 1.85, while k is 0.6 for barley and 0.583 for wheat. Substitution of these values into (13) yields values of s as given in Table 1.

As an example, I use a 70 cent per bushel rail rate and a cost factor of 1.85. These figures imply a truck/barge rate of 91 cents per bushel of wheat ($r/s = 70/.77 = 91$). The result is a 21 cent service quality (30 percent markup over the rail rate).

Comparison of revenue to variable cost ratios across similar shippers and of cost across competing modes are commonly followed practices in market dominance proceedings. The conceptual model yields two insights into railroad pricing policies. First, the value of competitive pressures can have a significant impact on rail prices as measured by the markdown from the monopoly price; in particular, markdowns are up to 40 percent for grain traffic. Second, even if competitive pressures are successful in reducing rail prices, the amount by which prices are reduced depends explicitly on the cost differential between the two modes and the relative value placed on service attributes. In particular, as the premium of other modes to rail (s) increases or as the marginal cost of rail increases relative to the other mode (MC_r/MC_t increases), the markup of the rail rate over marginal costs decreases.

To examine the magnitude of the latter effects, first consider the effect of an increase in the relative value of service attributes and then the effect of an increase in the relative costs of rail to other modes. Suppose $MC_r/MC_t = .5$, then if demanders view rail and the other mode as having comparable service attributes ($s = 1$), the inferred markup (i.e., $k = 1 - sMC_r/MC_t$) is equal to .5. But, if demanders instead view the relative value of the other mode's service attributes as being 20 percent higher than rail ($s = 1.2$) then the markup is .4. In this case, an increase in the value of service attributes results in a 20 percent reduction of the markup of rail rates over marginal costs. To evaluate the effects of changes in relative costs, suppose that demanders place a 20 percent premium on the other mode and relative costs change from .5 to .75. Then the markup of rail rate over marginal costs falls from .4 to .1. A 75 percent reduction in the markup of the rail rate over marginal costs.

V.   SUMMARY AND CONCLUSIONS

Legislation affecting regulation of the railroad industry (as well as other industries) has been toward increasing the emphasis on market fundamentals in the determination of rates. Although not totally deregulated, rail rates are subject to reasonableness scrutiny only if the railroad is market dominant over the route to which the rate applies. A finding of market dominance results from consideration of intramodal, intermodal, product, and geographic competition. The central contribution of this paper is an explicit representation of the market dominance criteria in a model of railroad pricing. This representation allows a simple explanation and interpretation of the regulatory rules. Specifically, the legislated market dominance standards map directly into a notion of shipper alternatives which yields an important conclusion. If the railroad is the low cost mode, the associated rate is either strictly market dominant or constrained market dominant. If strictly market dominant, rates are monopoly rates. If constrained market dominant, monopoly and competitive rates bound the rates chosen by railroads. The bound depends critically on the potential for demanders switching between alternatives in mode, product, and location. These are the focal points of the regulatory rules pertaining to market dominance.

The model is applied to the McCarthy Farms case in which the railroad was found to be market dominant and the rates unreasonable. Evidence from that case was used to evaluate the degree to which shipper alternatives restricted prices. Rail rates were found to be marked down by as much as 40 percent in markets with viable alternatives. Both cost and service attribute differentials were found to have a significant effect on the markup of rail rates from marginal costs.

Profit differences across shipper alternatives is the basis of this model and is also the basis for recent empirical research in transport demand. The latter research points to the value of service attributes as well as rates in determining the choices of shippers. As applied here, when differences in profit between transportation alternatives narrows, competitive pressures become more effective in constraining railroad market power. Yet, little research, if any, directly links these disaggregate studies of transport demand with a model of railroad pricing. Since the current emphasis in the industry is on negotiated rates between shippers and railroads, more research is necessary to evaluate the competitiveness of rates confronting shippers with discrete alternatives.

ACKNOWLEDGMENTS

Earlier versions of this paper were presented at the American Agricultural Economics Association meetings, the 7th World Conference of Transport Research, and in the Applied Microeconomics Workshop at the University of Oregon. I gratefully acknowledge useful comments and discussions from the audiences and from Kenneth L. Casavant, Kelly Eakin, Henry Goldstein, Jo Anna Gray, B. Starr McMullen, and William Wilson.

NOTES

1. The recently passed Interstate Commerce Commission Sunset Act of 1995 retains the existing market dominance standards and allow the newly formed Surface Transportation Board to consider other forms of transportation and economic alternatives in considerations of market dominance.

2.   Market dominance is term frequently used in antitrust proceedings on monopolization. Shepherd (1990a, 1990b, 1991), Dyer (1990), Flynn (1990) and Utton (1995) provide discussions of such proceedings. It is also often used to describe firms that have some degree of market power, the ability to set prices in excess of marginal cost. See, for example, Borenstein (1989, 1990), Dresner and Windle (1992), and Cabral and Riordon (1994).

3.   For in-depth summaries of the differing views of market dominance arguments, see Tye (1984a, 1984b), Eaton and Center (1985), Hauser and Grove (1986), and Robert D. Willig, Docket No. 372795, February 13, 1984.

4.   United States vs. E.I. duPont de Nemours Co., 3351 U.S. 377 (1956).

5.   See Winston (1983, 1985) for extensive reviews of the transportation demand literature. Also see Daughety and Inaba (1977) and Inaba and Wallace (1989).

6.   Willig, summarized in Tye (1984b), argues that all forms of competition affect demand elasticities. Consequently, the only form of competition relevant to market dominance is a specialized competitor serving only the traffic in question. Modal (intra- and inter-), product, and geographic competition are only relevant to the extent they prevent rates rising above stand-alone costs (e.g., the costs of a railroad providing only that service).

7.   ICC Docket Nos. 37809, 37809 (Sub-No. 1), and 37815S.

8.   The "just and reasonable" criterion was mandated by the Interstate Commerce Commission Act of 1887.

9.   Dalton and Redisch (1990) provide a review of the market dominance proceedings and recent cases following the 4-R Act and the Staggers Rail Act.

10.   Ex Parte No. 320, Special Procedures for Findings of Market Dominance, 353 ICC 874, modified, 355 ICC 12 (1976).

11.   A third criterion, not relevant to this paper, was whether shippers subjected to the rate had made substantial investments in rail equipment and/ or facilities rendering an absence of feasible transportation alternatives.

12.   Raab (1980) and Saving (1978) establish the result in the case of homogenous products using the dominant firm pricing model. Wilson, Wilson, and Koo (1988) extended that model to the case of differentiated products and applied the result empirically to the transportation industry.

13.   In 1980 the threshold was 1.6, rising to 1.8 in 1984, and currently the ratio depends on how close a railroad is to earning an adequate return on investment.

14.   Ex Parte No. 320 (Sub. No. 2), Market Dominance Determinations and Consideration of Product Competition, 365 ICC 118 (1981). Product competition as defined by the Act was sufficiently general to consider geographic competition as a component of product competition.

15.   However, the data are more difficult to obtain, and the demand model depends critically on identifying the decision maker, which is often difficult.

16.   Market dominance in an aggregate setting has been examined both theoretically and empirically by Wilson, Wilson, and Koo (1988).

17. Testimony of William Dempsey for the Association of American Railroads in hearings before the Subcommittee of Commerce, Science, and Transportation, Senate Commerce Committee, regarding S. 796, 96th Congress, 1st Session, May 22, 1979.

18. Inaba and Wallace (1989) theoretically and empirically characterize transport demand in such a supplier-based framework.

19. Firms face a wide variety of alternative production practices which can vary by the particular input used, as opposed to the quantity of the particular input used. For example, Wilson et al. (1986) investigate railroad pricing in a natural soda ash market for which a discrete alternative faced the receiving firm—synthetic soda ash.

20. For expository purposes, the discussion takes the receiver as the demander to choose the origin, and the supplier as the demander to choose the terminal market. However, in some cases the receiver may choose both the origin and destination, and the supplier may choose both the origin and terminal.

21. See Varian (1992) for discussion.

22. I simply use the McCarty Farms case to illustrate the model and its uses. To date, the McCarty Farms case, opened in 1980, remains open. The rates have been found to be the result of behavior in a market with a dominant firm and the rates unreasonable. Reparations to shippers have not been finalized. Dalton and Redisch (1990) describe the findings and status of a variety of other cases involving market dominance.

23. This assumption has been used previously, and has some obvious criticisms. For example, given prices are above the shutdown point, the use of average variable cost as opposed to marginal costs results in an overstatement of the Lerner Index which is used as a measure of control over price. For further discussion see Thompson (1982) and Tye (1984b).

24. In the model of the previous section, the Montana solution pertains to the strictly market dominant case ($\lambda = 0$) while the other region pertains to the constrained market dominant case ($\lambda > 0$).

25. This latter figure is comparable to estimates of Wilson et al. with regard to the impact of truck transportation on rail rates in North Dakota.

REFERENCES

Boyer, K.D. (1977). Minimum rate regulation, modal split sensitivities, and the railroad problem. *Journal of Political Economy, 85*(3), 493-512.

Borenstein, S. (1989). Hubs and high fares: Dominance and market power in the U.S. airline industry. *Rand Journal of Economics, 20*(3), 344-372.

Borenstein, S. (1990). Airline mergers, airport dominance, and market power. *American Economic Review, 80*(2), 400-404.

Cabral, L.M.B., & Riordan, M.H. (1994). The learning curve, market dominance, and predatory pricing. *Econometrica, 62*(5), 1115-1140.

Dalton, M., & Redisch, M. (1990). Coal transportation and the staggers rail act of 1980. In M.L. Aaranson, K. Kishna, D. Mahr, & T.M. Nechvatal (Eds.), *Fuel strategies, coal supply, dust control, and byproduct utilization.* New York: The American Society of Mechanical Engineers.

Daughety, A.F., & Inaba, F.S. (1977). *Empirical aspects of service differentiation and transportation demand* (Working Paper 601-7711). Northwestern University, Evanston, IL.

Dresner, M., & Windle, R. (1992). Airport dominance and yields in the U.S. airline industry. *Logistics and Transportation Review, 28*(4), 319-339.

Dyer, J.S. (1990). Legal approach to market dominance: Assessing market power in antitrust cases: Discussion. In J.R. Allison & D.L. Thomas (Eds.), *Telecommunications deregulation market power and cost allocation issues.* London: Greenwood, Quorum Books.

Eaton, J.A., & Center, J.A. (1985). A tale of two markets: The ICC's use of product and geographic competition in the assessment of rail market dominance. *Transportation Practitioners' Journal, 53*(1), 16-35.

Flynn, J.J. (1990). Legal approaches to market dominance: Discussion. In J.R. Allison & D.L. Thomas (Eds.), *Telecommunications deregulation market power and cost allocation issues.* London: Greenwood, Quorum Books.

Friedlaender, A.F., & Spady, R. (1980). A derived demand function for freight transportation. *Review of Economics and Statistics, 62*(3), 432-441.

Friedlaender, A.F., & Spady, R. (1981). *Freight transportation regulation.* Cambridge, MA: MIT Press.

Froeb, L.M., & Werden, G.J. (1992). The reverse cellophane fallacy in market definition. *Review of Industrial Organization, 7*(2), 241-248.

Hauser, K.L., & Grove, R.J. (1986). Competitive implications of the rail rate-to-cost ratio for export grain shipments. *Transportation Journal, 26*(2), 55-60.

Inaba, F.S. & Wallace, N.E. (1989). Spatial price competition and the demand for freight transportation. *Review of Economics and Statistics, 71*(4), 614-625.

Levin, R.C. (1978). Allocation in surface freight transportation: Does rate regulation matter? *The Bell Journal of Economics, 9*(1), 18-45.

McFadden, D., Winston, C. & Boersch-Supan, A. (1985). Joint estimation of freight transportation decisions under nonrandom sampling. In A. Daughety (Ed.), *Analytical studies in transport economics.* Cambridge, MA: Cambridge University Press.

Oum, T.H. (1979). A cross sectional study of freight transport demand and rail-truck competition in Canada. *Bell Journal of Economics, 10*(2), 463-482.

Raab, R.L. (1980). A note on dominant firm market structural economic Performance. *Review of Industrial Organization, 1*(1), 148-153.

Saving, T.R. (1978). Concentration ratios and the degree of monopoly. *International Economic Review, 11*(1), 139-146.

Shepherd, W.G. (1990a). The treatment of market dominance. *Review of Industrial Organization, 5*(2), 127-154.

Shepherd, W.G. (1990b). Section 2 and the problem of market dominance. *Antitrust Bulletin, 35*(4), 833-877.

Shepherd, W.G. (1991). Market dominance under U.S. antitrust. *Review of Industrial Organization, 6*(2), 161-176.

Thompson, M. (1982). The relevance of revenue/variable cost ratios to market dominance proceedings. *Transportation Research Forum-Proceedings, 23*(1), 362-368.

Tye, W.B. (1984a). On the effectiveness of product and geographic competition in determining rail market dominance. *Transportation Journal, 24*(1), 5-19.

Tye, W.B. (1984b). Revenue/variable cost ratios and market dominance proceedings. *Transportation Journal, 24*(2), 15-30.

Utton, M.A. (1995). *Market dominance and antitrust policy.* Aldershot, U.K.: Elgar.

Varian, H.A. (1992). *Microeconomic analysis* (3rd Ed.). New York: W.W. Norton and Co.

Wilson, W.W., Dooley, F., Griffin, G.C., & Casavant, K. (1986). The applicability of the theory of contestable markets to railroad competition. *Transportation Research Forum, Proceedings, 27*(1), 131-136.

Wilson, W.W., & Koo, W. (1988). Modal competition and pricing in grain transportation. *Journal of Transport Economics and Policy, 22*(3), 319-337.

Winston, C. (1981). A disaggregate model of the demand for intercity freight transportation. *Econometrica, 49*(4), 981-1006.

Winston, C. (1983). The demand for freight transportation: Models and applications. *Transportation Research, 17*(a), 419-427.

Winston, C. (1985). Conceptual developments in the economics of transportation: An interpretive survey. *The Journal of Economic Literature, 23*(1), 57-94.

THE RELATIVE BARGAINING POWER
OF PUBLIC TRANSIT LABOR

Ann Schwarz-Miller and Wayne K. Talley

ABSTRACT

Has government involvement in the transit industry enhanced the relative bargaining power of its labor? This question is investigated by comparing the wages of public transit bus drivers with those of private motor bus drivers and public nontransport operatives. The estimation results suggest that public transit bus drivers earned less than comparable labor groups in the private and public sectors in the pre-reform period (1977, 1979 and 1981), but their wages surpassed or equaled those of comparable labor groups in the post-reform period (1985 and 1990). Ironically, it was only after the advent of the Reagan Administration's policies to reduce transit labor costs that public transit bus drivers enjoyed a marked improvement in their relative wage status.

Research in Transportation Economics, Volume 4, pages 69-85.
Copyright © 1996 by JAI Press Inc.
All rights of reproduction in any form reserved.
ISBN: 1-55938-915-X.

I. INTRODUCTION

The typical U.S. transit firm (or system) is local-government-owned and receives subsidies from federal, state and local governments.[1] Although some argue that the public transit industry has benefitted from federal involvement, for example, maintaining and/or expanding services, others argue that this involvement has contributed to industry cost inefficiency. The Reagan Administration, in particular, held the view that transit operating subsidies were a wasteful allocation of government resources—financing higher transit wages, rather than improving or expanding service (Smerk, 1986). Consequently, the Administration lobbied Congress to eliminate federal transit operating subsidies, succeeding in having them reduced, in spite of Congressional resistance.[2] The Reagan Administration also sought to lower public transit costs by promoting the replacement of public transit services with lower-cost privately-provided services (i.e., contracting-out privatization):[3] Public transit systems were required to demonstrate that they were actively encouraging private firms to participate in the provision of transit services as a condition for the receipt of federal operating subsidies.[4]

Has government involvement in the transit industry enhanced the relative bargaining power of its labor? This question is investigated by comparing the labor earnings of the public transit industry with those of comparable labor in the private and public sectors. In the private sector comparison, we compare wages for a representative occupation, bus driver, found in both the public transit and the private bus (i.e., motor bus) industries. In the public sector comparison, we compare the wages of public transit bus drivers with those of public nontransport operatives. Transit bus drivers were selected because they represent the largest homogeneous labor group of transit bus service—the predominant service within the public transit industry. Motor bus drivers were chosen as a comparison group because their responsibilities and skills come closest to those of transit bus drivers. Public nontransport operatives also have skills similar to those of transit bus drivers and are not directly affected by the public transit environment.

The paper is structured as follows: Section II discusses the public transit industry and the effects (both theoretical and empirical) of government ownership and subsidization on transit wages. Government involvement in the motor bus industry is also discussed, providing information to construct (in the following section) the comparative wage equation for the two industries. Section III presents the data and the model for investigating the wages of public transit bus drivers relative to those of motor bus drivers. The estimation results comparing public transit and motor bus driver wages are detailed in Section IV, while the comparison involving public nontransport operatives is discussed in Section V. Conclusions are presented in Section VI.

II. PUBLIC TRANSIT AND MOTOR BUS INDUSTRIES

The public transit industry is highly unionized, with the majority of workers belonging to the Amalgamated Transit Union (ATU). The most significant features of government participation in the industry, public ownership and subsidization, are forces which potentially enhance the bargaining power of transit unions. It has been argued that unions in the public sector may inherently have more power than in the private sector, since wages are inextricably determined within an environment in which politicians respond to public workers as an organized lobbying and voting bloc with concentrated interests (see Fogel & Lewin, 1974; Reder, 1975).[5] In the public transit industry, this power not only lowers resistance to high wage demands, promotes the subsidization that helps to pay for them. A study by Hamermesh (1975) suggests that government (relative to private) ownership of the transit industry has had a positive effect on the wages of unionized transit bus drivers; support for the argument that operating subsidies augment wages of transit workers is found in studies by Pucher, Markstedt and Hirschman (1983) and Shughart and Kimenyi (1991).

The collective bargaining power of public transit unions has been protected and strengthened by Section 13(C) of the Urban Mass Transportation Act of 1964. Section 13(C) contains unique labor protection requirements regarding earnings, collective bargaining rights and job security as conditions for receiving federal subsidies, potentially providing transit unions with an advantage over other public sector unions (Gerhart, 1975). Transit management contends that this clause has given transit unions veto power over receipt of federal subsidies and therefore has served to expand labor demands (Talley, 1983, p. 306).

Transit policies initiated by the Reagan Administration should have reduced some of these advantages. The intent of contracting-out privatization was to lower the labor costs of transit services by substituting less expensive private sector labor for public workers. Union power to raise transit wages would then be limited by job losses and the desire to minimize further privatization of services (see Talley & Anderson, 1986; Talley, 1991). Declines in federal subsidies were also expected to contribute to lower union earnings. However, these effects were blunted by a dramatic increase in state and local government transit subsidies during the 1980s that more than offset the cutback at the federal level. In 1976, state and local government transit operating subsidies were $1.2 billion; by 1980 and 1983 they were $2.6 billion and $4.2 billion respectively. They subsequently increased from $5.4 billion in 1984 to $8.3 billion by 1990 (American Public Transit Association, 1992, p. 51).

Government involvement in the U.S. motor bus industry has typically taken the form of regulation. The motor bus industry is a multiservice transportation industry, consisting of privately-owned firms providing scheduled, regular route intercity passenger service; bus package express service; and various charter services. In 1935, the industry was placed under federal economic regulation with passage of the Motor Carrier Act, which gave the Interstate Commerce Commission (ICC) the authority to regulate prices, entry, exit, financial activities, and service levels of carriers engaged in interstate service.

By restricting market entry, regulation protected bus firms from competition and thereby improved the bargaining climate for bus unions. Historically, much of the industry's labor, like public transit labor, has been represented by the ATU. ICC regulation and the high degree of concentration in certain segments of the industry, for example, regular route intercity service, provided the

ATU with the opportunity to obtain a significant wage premium for union relative to nonunion workers. The ATU was particularly successful in exacting higher wage settlements from larger firms such as Greyhound that followed a policy of paying high wages and financing higher labor costs with price increases (see Fravel, 1991). However, faced with a continuing decline in its share of total U.S. intercity passenger traffic and a worsening financial performance, the industry in the late-1970s sought regulatory reform. The objective was to obtain flexibility to compete in the intercity passenger market to improve profitability.

Federal deregulation of the motor bus industry in 1982 through the Bus Regulatory and Reform Act (BRRA) provided pricing freedom and substantially reduced both entry and exit controls of the industry. The removal of pricing and entry restrictions coupled with a further decrease in the industry's share of intercity passenger travel placed competitive pressures on carriers to reduce labor costs. Evidence (see Schwarz-Miller & Talley, 1994) suggests that the wages of both union and nonunion motor bus drivers declined after deregulation.

III. PUBLIC TRANSIT VERSUS PRIVATE MOTOR BUS DRIVER WAGES—DATA AND MODEL

Current Population Survey (CPS) data (of the Bureau of the Census) for the years 1977, 1979, 1981, 1985, and 1990 are utilized to examine wage patterns in public transit compared with those in the motor bus industry.[6] The sample includes individual vehicle drivers providing for-hire bus service who worked 30 or more hours per week and provided information on usual weekly earnings, usual hours worked, union status, and a set of demographic characteristics.[7]

For both industries, the years 1977, 1979, and 1981 represent one distinct policy period and the years 1985 and 1990 represent another distinct policy period. For the former period, federal transit operating subsidies rose continuously and the motor bus industry operated in a regulated environment. For the latter period, transit systems were encouraged to privatize services and federal transit operating subsidies declined in real terms, while the motor bus industry operated in a deregulated environment. In the following discussion, the former period is referred to as the pre-reform period and the latter as the post-reform period.

We estimate an equation comparing transit and motor bus driver wages having the form

$$\ln W_{ij} = \Sigma \beta_k X_{ijk} + \alpha_1 UNION_{ij} + \alpha_2 PUB_{ij} + \alpha_3 UPUB_{ij}$$
$$+ \alpha_4 REF_{ij} + \alpha_5 UREF_{ij} + \alpha_6 PUBREF_{ij} \qquad (1)$$
$$+ \alpha_7 UPUBREF_{ij} + \epsilon_{ij},$$

where the index i represents the ith individual; j represents the jth year; and lnW is the natural log of hourly earnings in 1982-1984 dollars.[8] $UNION$ is a binary variable equal to 1 if the driver belongs to a union; PUB is a binary variable equal to 1 if the driver is a transit driver and zero for a motor bus driver; $UPUB$ is an interaction binary variable equal to 1 when the driver is an union transit driver; REF is a binary variable equal to 1 in the post-reform period (1985 and 1990) and zero in the pre-reform period (1977, 1979, and 1981); $UREF$ is an interaction binary variable equal to 1 for union drivers in the post-reform period; $PUBREF$ is an interaction binary variable equal to 1 when the driver is a transit driver in the post-reform period; $UPUBREF$ is an interaction binary variable equal to 1 when the driver is an union transit driver in the post-reform period; and ϵ is a stochastic error term with zero mean and constant variance. The control vector X includes a constant ($X_0 = 1$) and k variables measuring years of schooling completed ($SCHOOL$); years of experience, approximated as $AGE - SCHOOL - 5$, and years of experience squared/100 (EX and EXS); and binary variables equal to 1 if the driver is white ($WHITE$); married ($MARRIED$); male ($MALE$); or working in the Northeast ($NORTHEAST$), South ($SOUTH$) or West ($WEST$), as opposed to working in the North Central region of the country.

In equation (1) the union-nonunion log wage differential for motor bus drivers in the pre-reform period is measured by α_1; the log wage differential between nonunion transit bus drivers and nonunion motor bus drivers in the pre-reform period is measured by α_2; the difference between the transit driver and the motor bus driver union-nonunion log wage differential in the pre-reform period is measured by α_3; the log wage differential for nonunion motor bus drivers in the post-reform period relative to the pre-reform period by α_4; the change in the union-nonunion log wage differential for motor bus drivers in the post-reform period relative to the pre-reform period by α_5; the change in the log wage differential between nonunion transit drivers and nonunion motor bus drivers in the post-reform period by α_6; and the change in the difference between the transit driver and the motor bus driver union-nonunion log wage differential in the post-reform period by α_7.

For the purpose of this study, we are primarily interested in two sums of coefficients, that is, $\alpha_2 + \alpha_3$ and $\alpha_2 + \alpha_3 + \alpha_6 + \alpha_7$. The former is the log wage differential between union transit drivers and union motor bus drivers in the pre-reform period; the latter sum is the log wage differential between union transit and union motor bus drivers in the post-reform period. If these sums are positive, suggesting higher wages for union transit than for union motor bus drivers, we would have evidence (for both periods) of wage distortion and greater relative bargaining power in the public transit industry.

An alternate form of equation (1) including a set of four unemployment variables is also estimated to ensure that the time period binary variables are not picking up the effects of varying economic conditions:

$$\ln W_{ij} = \Sigma \beta_k X_{ijk} + \alpha_1 UNION_{ij} + \alpha_2 PUB_{ij} + \alpha_3 UPUB_{ij} + \alpha_4 REF_{ij}$$
$$+ \alpha_5 UREF_{ij} + \alpha_6 PUBREF_{ij} + \alpha_7 UPUBREF_{ij}$$
$$+ \alpha_8 UNEM_{ij} + \alpha_9 UUNEM_{ij} + \alpha_{10} PUBUNEM_{ij} \qquad (2)$$
$$+ \alpha_{11} UPUBUNEM_{ij} + \epsilon_{ij},$$

In this equation $UNEM$ is the regional unemployment rate[9] and UUNEM, PUBUNEM and UPUBUNEM are interaction binary variables equal to the regional unemployment rate when the driver

is (a) in a union, (b) a public transit driver and (c) a unionized
public transit driver, respectively.

A specification drawback of equation (1) is that the effect of
federal, state and local transit operating subsidies on the wage
differential between transit and motor bus drivers is not directly
addressed. As a final step, we address this drawback by modeling
this equation's PUB and $UPUB$ coefficients α_2 and α_3 as functions
of these subsidies, that is,

$$\alpha_2 = \alpha_{20} + \alpha_{21}FSL_j \qquad\qquad (3)$$

$$\alpha_3 = \alpha_{30} + \alpha_{31}FSL_j, \qquad\qquad (4)$$

where FSL_j represents the sum of federal, state and local
government transit operating subsidies for the jth year.[10] The
coefficient α_{21} measures the effect of a million dollar increase in
government transit operating subsidies on the log wage differential
between nonunion transit bus drivers and nonunion motor bus
drivers. The coefficient α_{31} measures the effect of a million dollar
increase in government transit operating subsidies on the
difference between the transit driver and motor bus driver union-
nonunion log wage differential. Substituting equations (3) and (4)
into equation (1) and rewriting, we obtain the following equation
to be estimated:

$$\ln W_{ij} = \Sigma_k B_k X_{ijk} + \alpha_1 UNION_{ij} + \alpha_{20}PUB_{ij} + \alpha_{21}FSL_j{}^*PUB_{ij}$$
$$+ \alpha_{30}UPUB_{ij} + \alpha_{31}FSL_j{}^*UPUB_{ij} + \alpha_4REF_{ij} \qquad\qquad (5)$$
$$+ \alpha_5UREF_{ij} + \alpha_6PUBREF_{ij} + \alpha_7UPUBREF_{ij} + \epsilon_{ij}.$$

IV. PUBLIC TRANSIT VERSUS PRIVATE MOTOR BUS
DRIVER WAGES—ESTIMATION RESULTS

Results from estimation of equation (1) are presented in Table 1.
The results show that in the pre-reform period, the union and
nonunion wages of motor bus drivers were higher than those of
transit drivers. In the post-reform period, however, the position

Table 1. Wage Equation Estimation Results:
Public Transit vs. Private Motor Bus Drivers

Variable	Coefficient
Constant	1.622*
	(0.143)
SCHOOL	0.005
	(0.008)
EX	0.019*
	(0.005)
EXS	-0.040*
	(0.009)
WHITE	-0.054
	(0.033)
MARRIED	-0.049
	(0.033)
MALE	0.190*
	(0.033)
NORTHEAST	0.092**
	(0.041)
SOUTH	0.079***
	(0.043)
WEST	0.088**
	(0.043)
UNION	0.352*
	(0.077)
PUB	-0.267*
	(0.075)
UPUB	0.158
	(0.100)
REF	-0.186*
	(0.068)
UREF	0.071
	(0.086)
PUBREF	0.413*
	(0.106)
UPUBREF	-0.241***
	(0.133)
R^2	0.449
$\bar{R}^2$	0.433
n	585

Notes: *(**,***) significant at the 1(5,10) percent level.
Standard errors are in parentheses; n is the sample size.

of transit drivers improved: Both union and nonunion wages of transit drivers exceeded those of motor bus drivers.

The coefficient of *PUB* (−0.267) is highly significant and negative, suggesting that nonunion transit drivers earned 23 percent less than nonunion motor bus drivers in the pre-reform period.[11] Although that coefficient of *UPUB* is positive, the sum of the coefficients of *PUB* and *UPUB* (i.e., $\alpha_2 + \alpha_3$) is negative and indicates that union transit drivers earned 10 percent less than union motor bus drivers in the pre-reform period. Using mean values of the demographic variables, hourly wages of unionized transit drivers are estimated at $10.00 and these of nonunion transit drivers at $6.00 for the pre-reform period. The coefficient of *PUBREF* (0.413) is positive and significant; the sum of the *PUB* and *PUBREF* coefficients (0.146) is also positive, implying that the wages of nonunion transit drivers surpassed those of nonunion motor bus drivers in the post-reform period by 16 percent. The sum of the coefficients of *PUB*, *UPUB*, *PUBREF* and *UPUBREF* (i.e., $\alpha_2 + \alpha_3 + \alpha_6 + \alpha_7$) is positive, indicating that the wages of union transit drivers exceeded those of union motor bus drivers by about 6 percent in the post-reform period. Hourly wages in the post-reform years are estimated at $10.58 for union transit drivers and $7.53 for nonunion transit drivers.

Collectively, the results clearly suggest that public transit bus drivers were not overpaid in the pre-reform period, at least not when compared with one of their closest peer groups, private motor bus drivers. Apparently, the lack of strong competition in the private sector prior to motor bus deregulation proved a much stronger force in maintaining earnings than did the transit industry's institutional factors for raising public transit wages, inspite of deteriorating demand in both sectors. The results further suggest that the relative position of transit drivers strengthened during the post-reform period, despite the Administration's objective of reducing public transit labor costs.

The estimate of equation (2), which utilized a set of unemployment variables to ensure that the time period changes were not simply reflecting business cycle forces, reinforces the original results (see the second column of Table 2). Based on the same variables or combinations of variables used in the equation

Table 2. Partial Wage Equation Estimation Results:
Public Transit vs. Private Motor Bus Drivers

Variable	Coefficient	Coefficient
UNION	0.094	0.352*
	(0.277)	(0.077)
PUB	-0.176	-0.186
	(0.323)	(0.234)
UPUB	-0.095	0.416
	(0.419)	(0.347)
REF	-0.208*	-0.187*
	(0.074)	(0.068)
UREF	0.101	0.072
	(0.919)	(0.086)
PUBREF	0.432*	0.482**
	(0.110)	(0.211)
UPUBREF	-0.241***	0.007
	(0.138)	(0.320)
UNEM	-0.023	
	(0.029)	
UUNEM	0.037	
	(0.038)	
PUBUNEM	-0.015	
	(0.046)	
UPUBUNEM	0.038	
	(0.059)	
FSL*PUB		-0.00002
		(0.00006)
FSL*UPUB		-0.00008
		(0.00009)
R^2	0.452	0.451
$\bar{R}^2$	0.433	0.433
n	585	585

Notes: *(**,***) significant at the 1(5, 10) percent level.
Standard errors are in parentheses; n is the sample size.

(1), the results again show: (1) both nonunion and union transit drivers earning less than their private bus counterparts in the pre-reform period (16 percent and 24 percent, respectively); and (2) a substantial improvement for nonunion transit drivers (25 percent), along with a small increase for union transit drivers (8 percent), holding unemployment constant, in the post-reform period.

Results from estimation of equation (5), the alternative form of equation (1) that includes the two interaction binary variables $FSL*PUB$ and $FSL*UPUB$, are presented in the third column of Table 2. The coefficients of these two variables are insignificant and virtually nothing is added to the explanatory power of the equation. The insignificance of the subsidy variables is in all likelihood a result of the (necessarily) highly-aggregative nature of the data. The central conclusion of the prior two equations—that the position of transit bus drivers improved relative to private drivers during the post-reform years—remains intact.

V. PUBLIC TRANSIT VERSUS PUBLIC NONTRANSPORT OPERATIVE WAGE—ESTIMATION RESULTS

How do the wages of public transit bus drivers compare with the wages of comparable labor in the public sector? We investigate this question by reestimating equation (1) using public nontransport operatives (rather than motor bus drivers), a comparable group of public sector labor not subject to any sweeping public policy changes over the observation period.[12, 13] As in the previous estimations, we utilize CPS data for the years 1977, 1979, 1981, 1985, and 1990.

The reestimation of equation (1) (see Table 3) reveals results similar to those found in the previous estimate of equation (1): In particular, the coefficient of PUB (-0.273), significant at the 10 percent level, implies a 24 percent wage disadvantage for nonunion public bus drivers relative to their public nontransport operatives counterpart in the pre-reform period. The sum of the coefficients of PUB and $UPUB$ (i.e., $\alpha_2 + \alpha_3$) is negative, indicating that union transit drivers earned 17.7 percent less than union public

Table 3.   Wage Equation Estimation Results:
Public Transit vs. Public Nontransport Operatives

Variable	Coefficient
Constant	-0.118
	(0.258)
SCHOOL	0.105*
	(0.014)
EX	0.034*
	(0.010)
EXS	-0.056*
	(0.018)
WHITE	-0.049
	(0.072)
MARRIED	0.239*
	(0.073)
MALE	0.265*
	(0.075)
NORTHEAST	0.054
	(0.095)
SOUTH	-0.017
	(0.087)
WEST	0.135
	(0.090)
UNION	0.367**
	(0.183)
PUB	-0.273***
	(0.142)
UPUB	0.078
	(0.211)
REF	-0.222
	(0.139)
UREF	0.133
	(0.232)
PUBREF	0.423**
	(0.192)
UPUBREF	-0.280
	(0.282)
R^2	0.422
$\bar{R}^2$	0.394
n	347

Notes: *(**,***) significant at the 1(5,10) percent level.
Standard errors are in parentheses; n is the sample size.

nontransport operatives in the pre-reform period. By contrast, the coefficient of *PUBREF* (0.423) is positive and significant; the sum of the coefficients of *PUB* and *PUBREF* (0.150) is also positive, indicating that the wages of nonunion transit drivers surpassed those of nonunion public nontransport operatives in the post-reform period by 16 percent. The sum of the coefficients of *PUB*, *UPUB*, *PUBREF* and *UPUBREF* (i.e., $\alpha_2 + \alpha_3 + \alpha_6 + \alpha_7$) is negative but relatively small, indicating that the wages of union transit drivers were approximately the same as the wages of union public nontransport operatives in the post-reform period, that is, the position of transit drivers strengthened during the post-reform period.[14]

The improvement in the relative wages of public transit bus drivers in the post-reform period appears to be the net outcome of inconsistent policies at the federal vs. state and local levels with respect to cost containment in public transit. Far stronger policy steps than those undertaken at the federal level would have been necessary to limit the relative improvement in public transit wages.

VI.   CONCLUSION

Has government involvement in the transit industry enhanced the relative bargaining power of its labor? This question was investigated by comparing the wages of public transit bus drivers with those of private motor bus drivers. Public transit driver wages were also compared with those of a more broadly-comparable public sector group—public nontransport operatives.

Our results suggest no systematic overpayment of wages to public transit labor relative to the wages of private motor bus labor and public nontransport operatives in the pre-reform period (1977, 1979, and 1981). In fact wages were found to be significantly lower, implying that transit operating subsidies and other characteristics of the public transit industry did not generate a net wage advantage for public transit drivers relative to comparable labor groups. By contrast, public transit wages surpassed or equaled those of comparable labor groups in the post-reform period (1985 and 1990). Ironically, it was only after the advent of the Reagan

Administration's policies to reduce transit labor costs that public transit bus drivers enjoyed a marked improvement in their relative wage status.

NOTES

1.   Until the 1960s transit firms were generally privately owned, operating under exclusive franchises subject to government regulation of fares and routes. However, a sharp deterioration in ridership, resulting from rising incomes and private automobile use, threatened the solvency of many systems, precipitating a trend of public takeover. During the 1960-1969 period, 21 transit systems in the 117 largest cities came under public ownership (Pashigan, 1976). By the early 1980s, 144 of the 159 largest systems were operated under public ownership (U.S. Department of Transportation, 1986). Federal transit capital and operating subsidies began with passage of the Urban Mass Transportation Act of 1964 and the National Mass Transportation Assistance Act of 1974, respectively.

2.   In 1976 federal transit operating subsidies were $442.9 million, reaching a peak of $1.1 billion in both 1980 and 1981, but declining to $827 million by 1983. In the years that followed (until 1990), these subsidies were relatively stable nominally, but declined 11.9 percent in real (measured in 1982-1984 dollars) terms (see *Transit Fact Book*, 1992, p. 51).

3.   Privatization of public transit service may include: (1) the sale of a public transit firm to the private sector or (2) the contracting-out of a service to the private sector. The latter type of privatization has generally been adopted in the United States. Contracting-out is the process by which the public transit firm and a private provider enter into a contract that gives the latter the exclusive right to provide a service. By replacing the public transit service with the lower-cost privately-provided service, the transit firm incurs cost savings. In addition to these cost savings, Talley (1991) also found evidence that cost savings may occur for the remaining non-contracted-out services of the firm: The transit firm's union, fearful of additional job losses, may agree to the elimination of a number of costly work rules as well as to a lower wage scale in order to limit further contracting-out of service. For further discussion of contracting-out (or privatization) of public transit service, see Talley and Anderson (1986), Meyer and Gomez-Ibanez (1991) and Black (1991).

4.   The policy of the Urban Mass Transportation Administration (UMTA) "charged localities with the responsibility of demonstrating that they were actively encouraging private firms to participate in the provision of new and restructured local services beginning in 1984. Unless UMTA was satisfied on this score, localities would not be able to obtain or retain matching funds for these services" (Sclar et al., 1989, p. 9).

5.   However, such countervailing factors as government budget and tax constraints tend to limit the power of public sector unions.

6.   The 1977, 1979, and 1981 data were taken from May CPS tapes; the 1985 and 1990 data were taken from 12-month CPS tapes. Twelve-month CPS tapes in which the union question was asked were not available prior to 1983.

7.   For this study, CPS data have two shortcomings: First, the CPS survey typically does not collect information on respondents' employers; thus, the study is unable to control for firm characteristics. Second, CPS data contain labor earnings, but not benefits; ideally an analysis of the total compensation packages of earnings and benefits would have been preferred.

8.   Hourly earnings are the ratio of "usual weekly earnings" divided by "usual hours worked per week" deflated via the Consumer Price Index (CPI).

9.   UNEM data are the unemployment rates for the four regions of this study and are taken from the U.S. Bureau of Labor Statistics, *Geographic Profile of Employment and Unemployment* (for various years).

10.   The variable FSL is the annual sum of federal, state and local government transit operating subsidies (taken from the *Transit Fact Book*) deflated using the Consumer Price Index (CPI). These data are not available by region or state. The variable *FSL* was also separated into two subsidy variables, *F* (federal operating subsidies) and *SL* (state and local operating subsidies). However, no appreciable change in the estimation results could be ascertained.

11.   Differentials are calculated as $(e^{\alpha} - 1) \cdot 100$.

12.   The selected nontransport operatives (from the CPS tapes) are workers in the following occupational categories: lathe and turning machine operators (704), welders and cutters (783), and production inspectors and examiners (796), where the numbers in parentheses are occupational codes of the U.S. Department of Commerce. These nontransport operatives were used as a control group by Hirsch (1988) in a truck driver earnings study.

13.   The equations that contain the subsidy and the set of unemployment variables have not been reestimated due to the statistical insignificance of these added variables in explaining wage rates.

14.   These results reinforce earlier findings by Schwarz-Miller and Talley (1995) using the same public control group, but a different sample, that public transit workers improved their relative wages during the post-reform period.

REFERENCES

American Public Transit Association. (1992). *Transit fact book*. Washington, DC: American Public Transit Association.

Black, A. (1991). Privatization of urban transit: A different perspective. *Transportation Research Record*, (1297), 69-75.

Fogel, W., & Lewin, D. (1974). Wage determination in the public sector. *Industrial and Labor Relations Review, 27*(3), 410-431.

Fravel, F.D. (1991). *Background paper on accessibility for the disabled and the intercity bus industry*. Washington, DC: U.S. Government Printing Office.

Gerhart, P.F. (1975). The effect of government ownership on union wages: Comments. In D.S. Hamermesh (Ed.), *Labor in the public and nonprofit sectors* (pp. 256-263). Princeton, NJ: Princeton University Press.

Hamermesh, D.S. (1975). The effect of government ownership on union wages. In D.S. Hamermesh (Ed.), *Labor in the public and nonprofit sectors* (pp. 227-255). Princeton, NJ: Princeton University Press.

Hirsch, B.T. (1988, Summer). Trucking regulation, unionization, and labor earnings: 1973-85. *Journal of Human Resources, 23*, :296-319.

Meyer, J.R., & Gomez-lbanez, J.A. (1991). Transit bus privatization and deregulation around the world: Some perspectives and lessons. *International Journal of Transport Economics, 18*(3), 231-258.

Pashigian, B.P. (1976). Consequences and causes of public ownership of urban transit systems. *Journal of Political Economy, 84*(6), 1239-1259.

Pucher, J., Markstedt, A., & Hirschman, I. (1983). Impacts of subsidies on the costs of urban public transport. *Journal of Transport Economics and Policy, 17*(2), 155-176.

Reder, M.W. (1975). The theory of employment and wages in the public sector. In D.S. Hamermesh (Ed.), *Labor in the public and nonprofit sectors* (pp. 1-48). Princeton, NJ: Princeton University Press.

Schwarz-Miller, A., & Talley, W.K. (1994). Motor bus labor earnings in regulated and deregulated environments. In S. McMullen (Ed.), *Research in Transportation Economics* (Vol. 4, pp. 95-117). Greenwich, CT: JAI Press Inc.

Schwarz-Miller, A., & Talley, W.K. (1995). Public transit wage rates: Pre-Reagan and Reagan-Bush eras. *Journal of Labor Research, 16*(2), 149-169.

Sclar, E.D., Schaeffer, E.H., & Brandwein, R. (1989). *The emperor's new clothes: Transit privatization and public policy.* Washington, DC: Economic Policy Institute.

Shughart II, W.F., & Kimenyi, M.S. (1991). *Public choice. Public subsidies. and public transit.* Washington, DC: U.S. Government Printing Office.

Smerk, G.M. (1986). Urban mass transportation: From private to public to privatization. *Transportation Journal, 26*(1), 83-91.

Talley, W.K. (1983). *Introduction to transportation.* Cincinnati, OH: South-Western Publishing Company.

Talley, W.K. (1991). Contracting out and cost economics for a public transit firm. *Transportation Quarterly, 45*(3), 409-420.

Talley, W.K., & Anderson, E. (1986). An urban transit firm providing transit, paratransit, and contracted out services: A cost analysis. *Journal of Transport Economics and Policy, 20*(3), 353-368.

U.S. Bureau of Labor Statistics. (Various Years). *Geographic profile of employment and unemployment.* Washington, DC: U.S. Government Printing Office.

U.S. Department of Transportation, Urban Mass Transportation Administration. (1986). *National urban mass transportation statistics: 1984 section 15 annual report.* Washington, DC: U.S. Government Printing Office.

A TRANSACTIONS CHOICE MODEL FOR FORECASTING DEMAND FOR ALTERNATIVE-FUEL VEHICLES

David Brownstone, David S. Bunch,

Thomas F. Golob, and Weiping Ren

ABSTRACT

The vehicle choice model developed here is one component in a micro-simulation demand forecasting system being designed to produce annual forecasts of new and used vehicle demand by vehicle type and geographic area in California. The system will also forecast annual vehicle miles traveled for all vehicles and recharging demand by time of day for electric vehicles. The choice model specification differs from past studies by directly modeling vehicle transactions rather than vehicle holdings. The model is calibrated using stated preference data from a new study of 4,747 urban

Research in Transportation Economics, Volume 4, pages 87-129.
ISBN: 1-55938-915-X.

California households. These results are potentially useful to public transportation and energy agencies in their evaluation of alternatives to current gasoline-powered vehicles. The findings are also useful to manufacturers faced with designing and marketing alternative-fuel vehicles as well as to utility companies who need to develop long-run demand-side management planning strategies.

I. BACKGROUND

Manufacturers and government agencies' are increasingly interested in promoting alternative-fuel vehicles. This is especially important in states like California, where stringent vehicle emission standards have been adopted or proposed. All new cars sold in California will be required to emit 80 percent fewer hydrocarbons and 50 to 75 percent fewer carbon monoxides and nitrogen oxides by the year 2000. At one time, the California Air Resources Board (CARB) also mandated the production and sale of zero-emission (electric) vehicles, beginning with 2 percent of annual sales in 1998 and increasing to 10 percent in 2003.

Since alternative-fuel vehicles, particularly electric vehicles, do not yet exist in the market, we need to use stated preference techniques to predict the demand for these vehicles. Previous studies have either ignored households' current vehicles and just modeled their choices over hypothetical vehicles, or they have tried to jointly model the choice of current and hypothetical vehicles (see the following literature review section for references) in a static framework. Since our primary interest here is forecasting, we will model the choice among hypothetical vehicles conditional on the vehicles currently held by the households. This approach captures the common sense notion that households do consider their current vehicle holdings when purchasing new vehicles. A major goal is to improve the quality of forecasts by focusing on vehicle transactions rather than vehicle holdings. By directly modeling transactions, we are able to forecast the diffusion of new alternative-fuel vehicles. In particular, we can predict what type and vintage of vehicles will be replaced by these new vehicles, which is a critical component in predicting the air pollution consequences from introducing alternative-fuel vehicles (see Kazimi, 1995).

II. LITERATURE REVIEW

A. Alternative-Fuel Vehicle Demand Models

Most of the earlier studies on alternative-fuel vehicle demand focused on demand for electric vehicles (EV's). The SRI (1978) study uses the model of Crow and Ratchford (1977) to forecast total sales of electric vehicles in the United States. Mathtech (Karfisi, Upton, & Agnew, 1978) forecasted electric vehicle demand by adapting a model in a Wharton Econometrics (1977) report. Beggs, Cardell and Hausman (1981) study the potential demand for EVs by applying an ordered logit model to stated preference data in which individuals provide rank orderings for hypothetical vehicle descriptions. Train (1980a) uses a vehicle-type choice model (multinomial logit model developed by Lave and Train (1979) to estimate the potential demand for EVs. Hensher (1982) focuses on the demand elasticities for electric cars in Sydney, Australia. Calfee (1985) studies only the potential private demand for electric autos (i.e., no trucks or vans), using discrete-choice SP data and a fully disaggregated logit model. Bunch et al. (1993) employ nested multinomial logit models and multinomial probit models for vehicle choice, and binary logit models for fuel choice.

Probably the most comprehensive forecasting work performed to date is that of Train (1986), which we describe here and in the next section. This work extends Train (1980b) and Lave and Train (1979) to forecast the market share for several specific non-gasoline-powered automobiles: three types of battery-powered vehicles (nickel-zinc, high-temperature #1, and high-temperature #2), a hybrid gas and battery vehicle, a hydrogen vehicle, and a vehicle run by the reaction of aluminum into energy and oxidation products. Train develops a "most likely case" scenario, and concludes that, for this scenario, 2.3 percent of passenger autos will be battery-powered by the year 2000. These results are similar to Dickson and Walton's (1977): they estimated that 3.4 million electric vehicles would be sold from 1990 to 2000, or about 2.4 percent of all vehicles sales during that period.

B. Vehicle Holdings and Transaction Models

There are many studies on vehicle holdings and transactions: see, e.g., the books by Train (1986) and Hensher et al. (1992) and references contained therein. The studies that are closest to our work are similar to Train (1986), so we summarize Train's model below.

Train (1986) develops a hierarchical structure to model auto ownership and use. This model has several submodels: a vehicle quantity submodel, a class/vintage submodel for one-vehicle households, a class/vintage submodel for two-vehicle households, an annual vehicle miles traveled (VMT) submodel for one-vehicle households, an annual VMT submodel for each vehicle for two-vehicle households, and submodels for the proportion of VMT in each of two categories (work and shopping) for one- and two-vehicle households, respectively.

Train's model has much in common with previous models: (1) it is a behavioral model that is estimated using choices from a household survey; (2) each household's choices depend on both vehicle class/vintage characteristics (such as vehicle purchase price) and household characteristics (such as household annual income); and (3) the model can be incorporated into a simulation framework to forecast the demand for and use of vehicles.

Compared to previous household vehicle demand models, Train's model has some advantages: (1) the model can forecast the number of vehicles owned and the annual VMT for each vehicle class/vintage; (2) it explicitly shows the interdependence between a household's choice of how many vehicles to own and its choice of which vehicle class/vintage to own; (3) it explicitly indicates that a household's choice of how many and what vehicle(s) to own closely relates to how much the household drives, and vice versa; and (4) it shows that each household chooses a particular make/model from within its chosen vehicle class without asking for a specification of the demand for each make/model.

Although there is a transaction dummy variable in Train's vehicle type submodel to take into account the generalized transaction costs associated with switching to a new vehicle portfolio, the model only predicts which class/vintage(s) a household will own at some point in time, without considering the transaction(s) leading to this portfolio. The model described in this paper is a dynamic model of household vehicle transactions. Since households change their vehicle holdings slowly, an explicit transactions model is necessary to accurately forecast households' responses to new alternative-fuel vehicles over the 10-15 year horizon most relevant to policy makers.

C. Combined Revealed Preference and Stated Preference Models

Since we need to measure households' preferences for alternative-fuel vehicles which are not currently available, we need to use responses to stated preference choice tasks in which households choose among hypothetical vehicle descriptions. Economists have been skeptical of stated preference data since they do not represent real choices in a market, and there have been few published attempts to compare forecasts from models calibrated using stated preference data to actual market behavior. Wardman (1988) reviews a number of studies comparing the forecasting ability of stated preference (*SP*) and revealed preference (*RP*) models of travel mode choice. He concludes that neither models generate good forecasts, but in some cases *SP* models were more accurate than *RP* models.

Many researchers have attempted to combine stated preference (*SP*) and revealed preference (*RP*) information to mitigate concerns about reliability of *SP* responses: Kroes and Sheldon (1988), Fowkes and Wardman (1988), Hensher, Barnard, and Truong (1988), Wardman (1988), Louviere (1988), Ben-Akiva and Morikawa (1990), and Bradley and Daly (1993). The most recent work by Morikawa (1994) and Hensher (1994) propose joint estimation of SP and RP choices allowing for the variances of the error term to differ.

Although we will use both *RP* and *SP* information, we will not estimate *RP* and *SP* choices jointly, but estimate *SP* vehicle choices conditioned on current *RP* holdings. Since the model we build will be used for one-step dynamic forecasting, using a conditional model incorporating all current information is appropriate. Forecasting *SP* vehicle choices by conditioning on *RP* vehicle holdings can also serve to capture some heterogeneity between households, therefore avoiding some possible bias problems.

III.   THE PERSONAL VEHICLE DEMAND MODEL

The framework for forecasting personal vehicle demand is summarized by the system diagram in Figure 1, which consists of a number of linked models. The initial current vehicle holdings and household structure are taken from the personal vehicle survey described below. Box A in Figure 1 represents a series of models which age each household by simulating births, deaths, divorces, children leaving home, and so forth. Once the new household structure is determined, other models in Box A determine the household's income and employment status. The dotted line leaving Box A shows that this updated household is used as the starting point for aging the household in the next period. The models in Box A are calibrated from the Panel Study of Income Dynamics (Hill, 1992), and their detailed specification is given in Kazimi (1995).

Ellipse B in Figure 1 takes the updated (aged) household and current vehicle holdings as inputs. It then decides whether or not a vehicle transaction takes place during this period. The simulation period length is set at six months so that the number of transactions occuring per period can be reasonably limited to one. However, model system outputs are reported annually. A vehicle transaction is defined to include: disposing of an existing vehicle, replacing an existing vehicle with another one, or adding a new vehicle to the household's fleet.

If the simulation from the transactions model in Ellipse B predicts that a vehicle transaction has taken place, the transaction

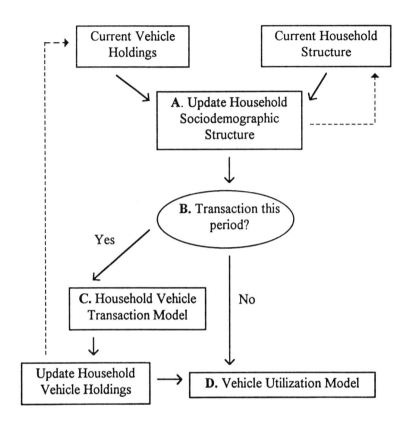

Figure 1. Personal Vehicle Submodel

type model in Box C determines exactly what type of transaction takes place. The household's vehicle holdings are updated accordingly, and these are used as starting values for the next period's simulation. The model outputs reported at the end of each year include estimates of vehicle totals by type and vintage. These are computed using choice probabilities taken over all possible actions to get weighted estimates. For new vehicles, this represents market penetration. The focus of this paper is on the model represented by Box C in Figure 1.

Another important component is utilization (model D). At the end of each year, it takes the updated vehicle holdings and household structure as inputs and then predicts the annual vehicle miles traveled for each household vehicle. For a more detailed discussion of this model, see Golob, Bunch, and Brownstone (1996). The usage forecasts are then converted to fuel demand by using average miles per gallon for liquid fuels and miles per equivalent gallons for non-liquid fuels. For electric vehicles, the utilization model also predicts the frequency of recharging at different times of day.

IV. THE SURVEY DATA

The survey used to calibrate the model in the next section was carried out in June and July, 1993. The sample was identified using pure random digit dialing and was geographically stratified into 79 areas covering most of urbanized California. An initial computer-aided telephone interview (*CATI*) was completed for each of 7,387 households. This initial *CATI* collected information on: household structure, vehicle inventory, housing characteristics, basic employment and commuting for all adults, and the household's intended next vehicle transaction.

The data from the initial CATI were used to produce a customized mail-out questionnaire for each sampled household. This questionnaire asked more detailed questions about each household member's commuting and vehicle usage, including information about sharing vehicles in multiple-vehicle and multiple-driver households. The mail-out questionnaire also contained two stated preference discrete-choice experiments for each household. Each of these experiments described three hypothetical vehicles, from which the households were asked to choose their preferred vehicle. These hypothetical vehicles included both alternative-fuel and gasoline vehicles, and the body types and prices were customized to include vehicles that were similar (but not identical) to the household's description of their next intended vehicle purchase.

After the households received the mail-out questionnaires, they were again contacted for a final *CATI*. This interview collected all the responses to the mail-out questions. Additional questions about the household's attitudes towards alternative-fuel vehicles were also included at the end of this interview.

The 4,747 households that successfully completed the mail-out portion of the survey in 1993 represent a 66 percent response rate among the households that completed the initial *CATI*. A comparison with Census data reveals that the sample is slightly biased toward home-owning larger households with higher incomes, and weights have been developed to balance the sample to the known population. Eighty percent of the households in the sample had exactly one driver per vehicle, showing that, in California, the number of drivers is the most important determinant of the vehicle ownership level. For two-vehicle households, a little over one-third of the vehicles are driven 10,000 miles per year or less, a third are driven 10,000 to 15,000 miles per year, and almost a third are driven more than 15,000 miles per year.

An example *SP* task from the questionnaire is given in the Appendix. There are four fuel-types for vehicles: gasoline, compressed natural gas (*CNG*), methanol, and electric (*EV*). Three of the four fuel-types appear in each *SP* question. For each fuel-type, two different body type versions are available. There were six (or seven) attributes per vehicle per choice set (depending upon the fuel type of the vehicle). Four levels were used to cover the range of most attributes, allowing for estimation of nonlinear effects. The basic experimental design used for producing variation in the attribute levels was an orthogonal main effects plan for a 4^{21} factorial in 64 runs (Golob et al., 1995). Respondents were spefically instructed to treat all non-listed attributes (e.g., maintenance costs and safety) as *identical* for all vehicles in the choice set.

V. MODEL SPECIFICATION

A. Variable Definitions

Any household vehicle transaction must fall into one of three categories: adding, replacing, or disposing. For adding or

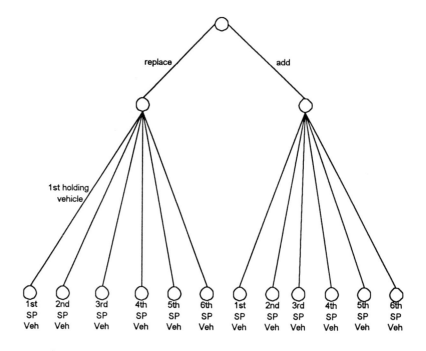

Figure 2.   One-Vehicle Household Transaction Tree

replacing, a household must decide which vehicle to add; for replacing or disposing, a household must decide which vehicle to dispose of. In our survey design, each household faces six vehicle choices containing a variety of fuel types, vehicle types, vehicle sizes, and other attributes. A household completing the stated preference survey in the Appendix could have 13, 20, or 27 transaction alternatives depending on whether its current number of vehicles is 1, 2, or 3, respectively. Figures 2 and 3 depict these alternatives for our models and they show all possible transactions each household type can carry out. For the present, zero-vehicle households are excluded, since there are only 53 households in the sample that own no vehicles.

The dependent variable specifications for the one- and two-vehicle households are provided in Tables 1 and 2, respectively. The order of the 1st and 2nd vehicles corresponds to the order

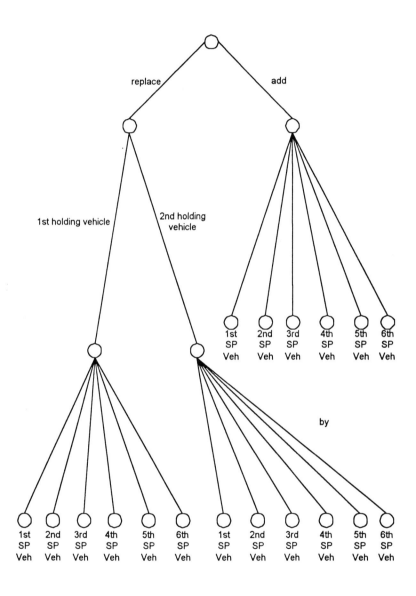

Figure 3. Two-Vehicle Household Transaction Tree

Table 1.   The Dependent Variable for
One-Vehicle Households

Value	Description
1	choose 1st SP vehicle to replace the held vehicle
2	choose 2nd SP vehicle to replace the held vehicle
3	choose 3rd SP vehicle to replace the held vehicle
4	choose 4th SP vehicle to replace the held vehicle
5	choose 5th SP vehicle to replace the held vehicle
6	choose 6th SP vehicle to replace the held vehicle
7	add 1st SP vehicle
8	add 2nd SP vehicle
9	add 3rd SP vehicle
10	add 4th SP vehicle
11	add 5th SP vehicle
12	add 6th SP vehicle
13	dispose of the held vehicle

in which respondents listed their vehicles. The order of SP vehicles one through six corresponds to the order on the survey form.

The estimates and forecasts described here do not distinguish between new and used SP vehicles. In the initial $CATI$ interview we asked respondents whether they intended to purchase a new or used vehicle at their next transaction, and we also asked the price range for the vehicle purchased as part of the next transaction. Future work will use these data to model the choice of new/used vehicles as well as the vintage of the used vehicles, but more accurate models require explicitly incorporating the choice of new or used vehicles into the stated preference design. Preliminary tests did not find any significant differences in preferences between new and used vehicle purchasers.

The model is intended to be used in a forecasting system, so all of the independent variables must either be exogenous to the forecasting system (e.g., vehicle attributes and fuel cost) or be an output from some other part of the forecasting system (e.g., household characteristics). This restriction eliminates potential variables such as home or work location, job classification, or commute distance. To avoid over-fitting (or "data mining") biases we did not repeatedly re-esimate models in an attempt to eliminate

Table 2.   Dependent Variable for
Two-Vehicle Households

Value	Description
1	choose 1st SP vehicle to replace the 1st held vehicle
2	choose 2nd SP vehicle to replace the 1st held vehicle
3	choose 3rd SP vehicle to replace the 1st held vehicle
4	choose 4th SP vehicle to replace the 1st held vehicle
5	choose 5th SP vehicle to replace the 1st held vehicle
6	choose 6th SP vehicle to replace the 1st held vehicle
7	choose 1st SP vehicle to replace the 2nd held vehicle
8	choose 2nd SP vehicle to replace the 2nd held vehicle
9	choose 3rd SP vehicle to replace the 2nd held vehicle
10	choose 4th SP vehicle to replace the 2nd held vehicle
11	choose 5th SP vehicle to replace the 2nd held vehicle
12	choose 6th SP vehicle to replace the 2nd held vehicle
13	add 1st SP vehicle
14	add 2nd SP vehicle
15	add 3rd SP vehicle
16	add 4th SP vehicle
17	add 5th SP vehicle
18	add 6th SP vehicle
19	dispose of the 1st vehicle
20	dispose of the 2nd vehicle

all insignificant coefficient estimates. Our primary interests are in the models' forecasts, not in the individual coefficient estimates.

We use the standard multinomial logit model to explain the discrete choices given in Tables 1 and 2, although we did carry out specification tests which are described in the next section. Since we are modeling the SP vehicle transaction choices conditioned on current vehicle holdings, attributes describing currently held vehicles enter the variables defining the utility scales corresponding to the discrete choices. For example, instead of entering the SP vehicle purchase price as an attribute, we enter the net capital cost associated with the entire transaction. This is defined as the SP vehicle purchase price minus the current market value of the held vehicle(s) for alternatives corresponding to replacing a vehicle; the SP vehicle purchase price for alternatives corresponding to adding a vehicle; and minus the current market value of the held vehicle for alternatives corresponding to disposing a vehicle. We use the same procedure to calculate net operating costs, top-speed and acceleration time.

The rationale for using these net benefit/cost variables is that a household not only compares the net gain or loss of a transaction, but also takes the benefit/cost left over from former holdings into account since this value does contribute to their utility. In other words, different remaining vehicles have different values to a household, so the utility function must include these factors.

Although these these variables are formulated based on transactions rather than on more traditional applications involving simple choices, they still retain the usual expected signs and interpretations. For example, since the net capital cost variable measures the capital cost associated with a vehicle transaction, all else equal households prefer to pay less for any transaction. Therefore we expect that this variable will have a negative coefficient in the utility function. For similar reasons, we expect that the coefficient of net operating costs will be negative, and the coefficient of the differences in top speeds will be positive.

B.   Testing the Independence of Irrelevant Alternatives

The multinomial logit specification used above assumes independently distributed Weibull disturbances in a random utility model. To test the validity of this specification, Hausman and McFadden (1984) show that if a subset of the choices is irrelevant, then eliminating it from the model will not systematically affect the underlying parameter estimates. However, excluding these choices will be inefficient. This is the basis for Hausman's specification test:

$$\chi^2 = (\hat{\beta}_r - \hat{\beta}_u)'[\hat{V}_r - \hat{V}_u]^{-1}(\hat{\beta}_r - \hat{\beta}_u), \qquad (1)$$

where β is the vector of coefficient estimates, matrix V is the estimate of the asymptotic covariance matrix, subscript r denotes estimators for the restricted subset, and u denotes estimators for the full set of choices. This statistic is asymptotically distributed as chi-squared with K degrees of freedom, where K is the rank of the weight matrix. In applying this test, a specific nominal choice alternative associated with an alternative-specific dummy variable might be eliminated from all choice sets. In this case, the coefficients for the alternative-specific dummy variable and any other variables that interact with this variable will not be identified in the restricted β vector. In this case only the remaining identified coefficients can be used to perform the test.

C.   Forecasting Methodology

Forecasts are generated using sample enumeration. Confidence bands for the forecasts are generated by parametric bootstrapping (see Efron & Tibshirani, 1993) as described below. In the most general case different models could be estimated for individual "market segments" in the population. Our forecasts are obtained using two models: one for one-vehicle households, and one for multiple-vehicle households. The following steps (with some notational details suppressed) summarize the procedure:

Step 1. Establish a scenario for the forecast year, for example, establish vehicle types and attributes for a hypothetical new vehicle market.

Step 2. Establish the $\hat{\beta}$ to be used.

Step 3. Using the scenario from step 1, establish transaction alternatives for each household in the sample. Using the $\hat{\beta}$ from step 2, compute choice probabilities for all transaction alternatives.

Step 4. Use equation 2 below to compute a consistent estimate of the population's average probability of choosing transaction alternative j:

$$\hat{S}_j = \frac{1}{N_p} \Sigma_{i=1}^{N} w_i P_{ij} (\hat{\beta}), \qquad (2)$$

where S_j is the forecast average probability of choosing alternative j in the population; N_p is the population size; N is the sample size; w_i is the household weight; and P_{ij} is the probability that household i chooses transaction alternative j.

Step 5. Compute a sales forecast for vehicles of a particular fuel-type. A transaction alternative is characterized by a transaction

type (add, replace, dispose), and for adds or replaces the type of
vehicle that has been purchased is also specified. So, to calculate
the demand probability for a particular fuel-type, one should
combine the appropriate transaction choice probabilities.

Step 6. Apply bootstrapping using steps 2 to 5; that is, based
on the initial estimates of $\hat{\beta}$ and its covariance matrix, randomly
draw $\hat{\beta}$ in step 2 and repeat the remaining steps. Do this hundreds
or thousands of times. Relevant statistics such as the median and
the 90 percent confidence bounds of $\hat{S}_j$ are then calculated using
these bootstrapped values.

VI.   PERSONAL VEHICLE DEMAND ESTIMATION RESULTS

Of 1607 one-vehicle households and 2220 two-vehicle households,
1153 and 1156 valid observations remained after excluding those
with missing or incorrect data, primarily household income and
vehicle year/make/model. Although the model specification could
be extended to three or more vehicle households, they are excluded
from this paper due to their small sample sizes. Due to lack of
data on vehicle attributes, we excluded all vehicles with model
years before 1979. Estimation results are obtained using data from
the first SP task for each sample household.

For easy comparison, the results for one- and two-vehicle
households are listed first and then the results are analyzed and
compared. Standard likelihood ratio tests show that the
coefficients from these two models are significantly different,
although preliminary tests cannot reject the hypothesis that the
two-vehicle household model holds for three-vehicle households
as well.

The estimation results for the sample of one-vehicle households
are listed in Table 3. The Hausman test described in the previous
section was computed for one-vehicle households by excluding the
replacement alternatives. At the 95 percent significance level, we
cannot reject the hypothesis that the multinomial logit
specification is correct.

Table 3. Estimation Results for One-Vehicle Households

Explanatory Variables	Coefficient	t-value
Net capital cost (HH income ≤ $30K, HH has a child of age < 21)*	-0.00003290	-1.1
Net capital cost (HH income ≤ $30K, HH has no child of age < 21)*	-0.00006952	-3.8
Value of the remaining vehicle (HH income ≤ $30K)*	0.00008264	2.4
Net capital cost ($30k < HH income ≤ $75K, HH has no children < 21)*	-0.00003925	-2.5
Value of the remaining vehicle ($30k < HH income ≤ $75K)*	0.00003080	1.3
Net capital cost (HH income > $75k, HH has a child of age < 21)*	-0.00005253	-1.5
Net capital cost (HH income > $75K, HH has no child of age < 21)*	0.00002766	1.3
Net operating cost(HH income ≤ $30K, HH has a child of age < 21)**	-0.008119	-0.2
Net operating cost (HH income ≤ $30K, HH has no child of age < 21)**	-0.08003	-3.3
Operating cost of the remaining vehicle (HH income ≤ 30K)**	-0.03190	-0.6
Net operating cost ($31K ≤ HH income ≤ 75K, HH has a child of age < 21)**	-0.1137	-3.1
Net operating cost ($31K ≤ HH income ≤ 75K, HH has no child of age < 21)**	-0.07709	-3.4
Net operating cost (HH income ≥ $76K, HH has no child of age < 21)**	-0.1252	-2.4
Top-speed difference between the *SP* vehicle and the held vehicle	0.0008844	0.5
Acceleration time diff. between the *SP* vehicle and the held vehicle***	-0.03713	-1.6
Refueling time of the *SP* vehicle	-0.0005721	-0.9
Range of the *SP* vehicle	0.006191	2.7
Range^2 of the *SP* vehicle	-0.000005299	-1.0
Service station availability for *EV*[†]	0.5736	1.2
Service station availability for dedicated *CNG* vehicle[†]	1.004	2.3
Service station availability for methanol vehicle and dual fuel *CNG* vehicle	0.2995	1.3
Luggage space of *SP* vehicle[††]	0.6246	1.8
Dual fuel (dummy)	0.2780	1.3
Pollution level of *SP* vehicle, for HH *with* child of age < 21[†††]	-0.5397	-1.8
Pollution level of *SP* vehicle, for HH *without* child of age < 21[†††]	-0.4637	-2.1
Van (HH size ≤ 3) (dummy)	-0.7891	-3.4

(continued)

Table 3.   (Continued)

Explanatory Variables	Coefficient	t-value
Van (HH size ≥ 4) (dummy)	0.7851	2.4
EV (Northern Calif. w/o SF, Oakland, San Jose) (dummy)	-0.1714	-0.6
EV*Subcompact (dummy)	0.2307	0.8
EV*Compact car (dummy)	0.2501	1.1
EV*Large (dummy)	0.4355	1.8
EV*Station Wagon (dummy)	-0.4104	-1.3
EV*Sport car (dummy)	0.3840	0.9
EV*Van (dummy)	-0.3092	-0.9
EV*Truck (dummy)	-1.042	-3.3
EV*Utility vehicle (dummy)	0.3604	0.8
CNG*Mid-size car (dummy)	0.05368	0.3
CNG*Large car (dummy)	-0.2283	-1.1
CNG*Station Wagon (dummy)	-0.8535	-3.0
CNG*Van (dummy)	0.6419	2.2
CNG*Utility (dummy)	2.004	6.0
CNG*Sport car (dummy)	1.011	3.0
Methanol*Mid-size car (dummy)	0.1497	0.9
Gasoline (dummy)	0.5947	2.0
Gasoline*Subcompact (dummy)	-0.1309	-0.5
Gasoline*Mini (dummy)	-1.180	-2.0
Gasoline*Compact (dummy)	-0.3851	-1.5
Gasoline*Mid-size car (dummy)	-0.3255	-1.3
Gasoline*Station Wagon (dummy)	-0.4900	-0.6
Gasoline*Van (dummy)	0.05017	0.2
Gasoline*Sport (dummy)	1.553	4.6
Gasoline*Utility (dummy)	0.5034	1.4
Gasoline*Truck (dummy)	-1.063	-4.5
New holding—two vans (dummy)	-0.9030	-1.2
New holding—two trucks (dummy)	0.7444	1.3
New holding—two utility vehicles (dummy)	-0.4545	-0.4
New holding—two station wagons (dummy)	-0.4900	-0.6
New holding—two cars (dummy)	0.1738	0.4
Alternative-add constant for HH with # cars < # drivers (dummy)	1.183	3.1
Alternative-add constant for HH, with children 15 or 16 years old (dummy)	0.7204	1.7
Alternative-add constant for HH with held vehicles type different from the SP vehicle's type	-0.1999	-0.5
Alternative-replace constant for HHs with # cars ≥ # drivers (dummy)	0.2207	0.6
Alternative-replace constant (replacing station wagon by van) (dummy)	0.6097	1.3
Alternative-replace constant for HHs with held vehicle's type the same as SP vehicle's (dummy)	1.4531	4.6

(continued)

Table 3.   (Continued)

Explanatory Variables	Coefficient	t-value
Alternative-dispose constant for Hhs with at least one member's age $\geq$ 60	1.359	3.8
Number of observations	1153	
Initial Likelihood	-2957.3866	
Final Likelihood	-2349.0719	
"Rho-Squared" w.r.t. Zero	0.2057	

Notes: HH stands for household; K stands for $1,000; # stands for number; and a dummy takes the value 1 when the condition is met, otherwise it is zero.

   * 1993 U.S. dollars.

   ** For *EV*, using home-refueling cost and home-refueling time. The unit for cost is cent/mile and the unit for refueling time is minutes. The gasoline price is assumed 120 cents/gallon.

   *** The time from 0 to 30 mph.

   † It is the proportion of service stations which carry the fuel.

   †† It takes the value of 1 (same size as *RP* vehicle) or .7 (30% smaller than *RP* vehicle).

   ††† It takes the value of 1 (1993 gasoline vehicle), or 0.4, 0.25, or 0 (for other alternative-fuel vehicles).

The two-vehicle household estimation results are listed in Table 4. The Hausman test was also computed for two-vehicle households by excluding the replacement alternatives. At the 95 percent significance level, we cannot reject the hypothesis that the multinomial logit specification is correct.

A.   Net Capital Cost

Net capital cost is defined as the difference between the price of the *SP* vehicle and the current market value of the held vehicle. Since this is just the capital cost of carrying out the transaction, we expect that the coefficient will be negative. Table 3 shows that net capital cost for one-vehicle households with annual income less than $75,000 has a coefficient with the expected negative sign. For households with annual income greater than $76,000 the coefficient for net capital cost is insignificant. Note that there are large differences (for both one and two-vehicle households) between households with and without children living at home.

For two-vehicle households with annual income less than $30,000, the results are very similar to the one-vehicle results in that both have a negative sign. However, for the two-vehicle

Table 4.   Estimation Results for Two-Vehicle Households

Explanatory Variables	Coefficient	t-value
Net capital cost (HH income ≤ $30K, HH has a child of age < 21)*	-0.0000706	-1.5
Net capital cost*(HH income ≤ $30K, HH has no child of age < 21)*	-0.00002882	-0.7
Value of the remaining vehicle (HH income ≤ $30K)*	0.0001215	2.2
Net capital cost (HH income > $30K, HH has a luxury vehicle and a child of age < 21)*	0.00002205	1.4
Net capital cost (HH income > $30K, HH has a luxury vehicle and no child of age < 21)*	0.00002118	1.8
Net capital cost (HH income > $30K, HH has no luxury vehicle, but a child of age < 21)*	-0.00001741	-1.0
Net capital cost (HH income > $30K, HH has no luxury vehicle & no child of age < 21)*	-0.00004112	-2.7
Value of the remaining vehicle (HH income > $30k, HH has no luxury vehicle)*	0.0001512	5.8
Net operating cost (HH income ≤ $30K, HH has a child of age < 21)**	-0.01004	-0.2
Net operating cost (HH income ≤ $30K, HH has no child of age < 21)**	-0.03318	-0.8
Net operating cost (HH income ≥ $31K, has luxury vehicles & a child of age < 21)**	-0.08157	-1.5
Net operating cost (HH income ≥ $31K, has a luxury vehicle & no child of age < 21)**	-0.08467	-1.9
Operating cost of the remaining vehicle (HH income > $30K, has a luxury vehicle)**	0.1963	3.1
Net operating cost (HH income > $30k, has no luxury vehicle, but a child of age < 21)**	-0.08214	-3.3
Net operating cost (HH income > $30k, has no luxury vehicle & no child of age < 21)**	-0.08404	-3.5
Operating cost of the remaining vehicle (HH income ≤ $30k, has no luxury vehicle)**	-0.01627	-0.4
Top-speed difference between the *SP* vehicle and the held vehicle	0.002398	1.6
Acceleration time difference between the *SP* vehicle and the held vehicle (HH income ≤ $30K)***	0.08322	1.6
Acceleration time of the remaining vehicle (HH income 30K)***	-0.2512	-1.4
Acceleration time difference between the *SP* vehicle and the held vehicle (HH income > $30K)***	-0.08143	-3.4
Acceleration time of the remaining vehicle (HH income ≤ $30k)***	-0.1905	-1.8
Refueling time of the *SP* vehicle	-0.0004997	-0.8
Range of the *SP* vehicle	0.005088	2.2
Range² of the *SP* vehicle	-0.00000127	-0.2

(continued)

Table 4. (Continued)

Explanatory Variables	Coefficient	t-value
Service station availability for EV[†]	0.5846	1.3
Service station availability for dedicated CNG vehicle w/o home-refueling[†]	0.7408	1.5
Service station availablity for dedicated CNG vehicle w/ home-refueling[†]	0.6312	1.2
Luggage space of SP vehicle[††]	0.4897	1.4
Dual fuel (dummy)	0.1136	0.8
Pollution level of SP vehicle for HH *with* child of age < 21[†††]	-0.2453	-1.1
Pollution level of SP vehicle for HH *without* child of age < 21[†††]	-0.02630	-0.1
Van (HH size ≤ 3) (dummy)	-0.07966	-0.4
Van (HH size ≥ 4) (dummy)	0.9119	4.7
EV*(LA & Orange Counties) (dummy)	-0.4391	-1.9
EV*(S.F., Oakland, San Jose) (dummy)	-0.2549	-1.1
EV*(Northern Calif. w/o SF, Oakland, and San Jose (dummy)	-0.1064	-0.4
EV*(Subcompact, Mini, Compact Cars) (dummy)	0.3935	1.7
EV*Mid-size car (dummy)	0.6481	2.6
EV*Sport car (dummy)	0.4521	1.0
EV*Van (dummy)	-0.4435	-1.7
EV*Truck (dummy)	-0.7238	-2.8
EV*Utility vehicle (dummy)	0.3357	0.8
CNG*Station Wagon (dummy)	-0.9945	-3.3
CNG*Van (dummy)	-0.2642	-1.1
CNG*Truck (dummy)	-0.6307	-2.6
CNG*Utility (dummy)	0.8466	2.7
CNG*Sport car (dummy)	0.8092	2.0
Methenol*Subcompact car (dummy)	-0.1107	-0.5
Gasoline*Subcompact (dummy)	-0.2140	-0.9
Gasoline*Mini (dummy)	0.7479	1.2
Gasoline*Compact(dummy)	-0.1091	-0.6
Gasoline*Large car (dummy)	-0.2788	-1.3
Gasoline*Station Wagon (dummy)	-0.9993	-3.3
Gasoline*Van (dummy)	-0.3276	-1.4
Gasoline*Sport (dummy)	0.1597	0.4
Gasoline*Utility (dummy)	0.7747	2.6
Gasoline*Truck (dummy)	-0.3948	-2.1
New holding—two or more vans (dummy)	-0.5580	-1.9
New holding—two or more trucks (dummy)	-0.07972	-0.3
New holding—two or more utility vehicles (dummy)	-0.2514	-0.5
New holding—two or more station wagons (dummy)	-0.3542	-0.7
New holding—two or more cars (dummy)	0.2489	2.5

(continued)

Table 4.   (Continued)

Explanatory Variables	Coefficient	t-value
Alternative-add constant for Hhs with # cars < # drivers (dummy)	0.3763	1.1
Alternative-add constant for Hhs with a child 15 or 16 years old (dummy)	0.8745	2.6
Alternative-add constant for HHs with held vehicle's type different from the *SP* vehicle's type	-0.4368	-2.6
Alternative-replace constant for HHs with # cars ≥ # drivers (dummy)	1.037	3.9
Alternative-replace constant*(Lower value vehicle) (dummy)	0.3618	3.7
Alternative-replace constant*(Replacing Station wagon by van) (dummy)	0.6508	2.0
Alternative-replace constant for HHs with held vehicle's type the same as *SP* vehicle's (dummy)	1.001	12.5
Alternative-dispose constant for Hhs with at least one member's age ≥ 60	1.447	3.7

Number of observations	1156
Initial Likelihood	-3463.0665
Final Likelihood	2880.1143
"Rho-Squared" w.r.t. Zero	0.1683

Notes: HH stands for household; K stands for $1,000; # stands for number; and a dummy takes the value 1 when the condition is met, otherwise it is zero.
  * 1993 U.S. dollars.
  ** For *EV*, using home-refueling cost and home-refueling time. The unit for cost is cent/mile and the unit for refueling time is minutes. The gasoline price is assumed 120 cents/gallon.
  *** The time from 0 to 30 mph.
  † It is the proportion of service stations which carry the fuel.
  †† It takes the value of 1 (same size as *RP* vehicle) or .7 (30% smaller than *RP* vehicle).
  ††† It takes the value of 1 (1993 gasoline vehicle), or 0.4, 0.25, or 0 (for other alternative-fuel vehicles).

households with income greater than $30,000, the result varies significantly between households with and without luxury cars. The households without luxury cars behave more like "rational" people in that their demand is a negative function of price. The households with luxury cars, however, prefer high-priced vehicles as reflected in the positive and significant coefficient. This result implies that there is a "name-plate" effect; that is, some people not only buy a vehicle but also buy status. This specification—with and/or without luxury vehicles—does capture some unobservable characteristics existing in the households.

B.   Net Operating Cost

Net operating cost is defined as the difference between the operating cost of the *SP* vehicle and the operating cost of the held vehicle(s). Net operating cost reflects the net amount of money that must be spent when a household uses the chosen vehicle. Except for two-vehicle households holding luxury cars, the coefficients of net operating costs for both one- and two-vehicle households have the expected negative sign. For two-vehicle households holding luxury cars and with income greater than $31,000, the coefficient for net operating cost is positive and significant, as it was for net capital cost. Coefficients also vary according to household income and with/without children under 21.

C.   Value and Operating Cost of the Vehicles in the Resulting Household Fleet

The value of the vehicles left in the household fleet after a particular transaction takes place represents an asset. Thus, we expect that the coefficients of "Value of remaining vehicle" should have a positive sign, and they do.

However, operating costs of all remaining vehicles still represent expenses, so the signs of the coefficients of "Operating cost of the remaining vehicle" should be negative. The results also support this expectation. The value and operating cost coefficients also varied with households' income and the presence of children under 21.

D.   Top Speed and Acceleration Time

The coefficients of the difference in top-speed have expected positive signs for both one- and two-vehicle households, which confirms that households prefer higher top speeds. However, the coefficient is insignificant for one-vehicle households, and is only marginally significant for two-vehicle households.

For the one-vehicle households, the coefficient of the difference in acceleration is marginally significant with the expected negative sign. For two-vehicle households, the coefficient for a household with income of $30,000 or less has a positive sign, and the coefficient for income of $31,000 or higher has an expected negative sign and is significant. Although it is not clear why the coefficient for a low-income household is positive, this does show that low-income households, in contrast to a high-income households, do not care too much about acceleration time. Acceleration time of the remaining vehicle for low- and high-income two-vehicle households have the expected negative coefficients.

E.   Refueling Time

Refueling time is defined as the service station refueling time for a non-*EV* and home-refueling time for an *EV*. For both one- and two-vehicle households the refueling time coefficients have the expected negative signs, but are not significant. Although *EV*s take much more time to refuel than do non-*EV*s, *EV* recharging occurs overnight at home so that the time requirement is not significant.

F.   Vehicle Range

As expected, the coefficient of range for both one- and two-vehicle households has a positive sign and is significant. This implies that range is an important factor when households buy an alternative-fuel vehicle. The coefficient for $(range)^2$ has a negative sign and is not significant. Although the coefficients of $(range)^2$ are not significant for both one- and two-vehicle households, the implication is important: the increase in value from increasing vehicle range declines.

G.   Service Station Availability

For both one-vehicle and two-vehicle households, the service station availability coefficients have the expected positive signs and their *t*-statistics range from 1.2 to 2.3. For two-vehicle households the coefficient for dedicated *CNG* vehicles without home-refueling is, as expected, the largest. Service station availability for dedicated *CNG* vehicles with and without home-refueling have the same value for one-vehicle households, so they are combined. For two-vehicle households, this coefficient is significant and relatively large in magnitude.

H.   Emissions Level

For both one- and two-vehicle households, these two coefficients have expected negative signs and are significant. Also, as expected, the coefficient for households with children has a larger negative value than that for households without children. This is especially so for two-vehicle households, where the coefficient for households with children under 21 years of age is almost 10 times greater than that of households without children. These results indicate that households with children are willing to pay for less-polluting vehicles regardless of fuel type.

I.   Vehicle and Fuel-Type Interactions

There are many significant interactions between vehicle type and fuel type in both the one- and two-vehicle models. These interaction terms imply preferences for particular vehicle fuel and body type combinations that cannot otherwise be explained by capital costs, operating costs, and range. To summarize, the results show that people are more likely to buy electric cars, as opposed to electric light-duty trucks and vans, and they are more likely to buy *CNG* utility and sport utility vehicles.

One-vehicle households generally prefer a gasoline vehicle to other alternative-fuel vehicles. For two-vehicle households this coefficient is zero; that is, for two-vehicle households a gasoline vehicle has no special advantage over alternative-fuel vehicles.

J.   Vans

For both one- and two-vehicle households, the coefficients of van dummy variables for household size greater than 3 are significant and have the expected positive signs. This implies that households with 4 or more people will be more likely to buy a van.

For one-vehicle households of size less than 4, the coefficient has an expected negative sign and is significant. For two-vehicle households the coefficient has an expected negative sign, but is not significant. This difference between one- and two-vehicle households implies that for households with 3 or fewer people the value of a van is much less for a one-vehicle household than for a two-vehicle household.

K.   Holdings of Two or More Vehicles of the Same Type

When a household decides to add a vehicle, a one-vehicle household will become a two-vehicle household and a two-vehicle household will become a three-vehicle household. We generally expect a household to have two or more cars, but not two or more special vehicles, such as two vans. For one-vehicle households these coefficients are not significant, but the coefficient associated with holding two trucks has an (unexpected) positive sign. For two-vehicle households, all the signs of the coefficients are as expected. The coefficients for new-holding-two-or-more-vans and for new-holding-two-or-more-cars are negative and significant.

L.   Households Adding Vehicles

For both one- and two-vehicle households, coefficients associated with adding vehicles in households with fewer vehicles than drivers, and in households with children 15 or 16 years old, have the expected positive signs and have t-statistics ranging from 1.1 to 3.1. Obviously, when a household has more drivers than cars, or has a child 15 or 16 years old (close to or at legal driving age), the household will be more likely to add a car.

The coefficient associated with households where the held vehicle type is different from the SP vehicle type variable is designed to determine if a household would like to add a vehicle which is different from their held vehicle. For one-vehicle households the coefficient is negative and not significant, which implies that one-vehicle households may or may not add a new vehicle that is different in type from the held vehicle; that is, any combination of two types of vehicle is possible. For two-vehicle households the coefficient is negative and significant, which implies that it is unlikely for a two-vehicle household to add a new vehicle that is different in type from both held vehicles; that is, a three-vehicle household is unlikely to have, for example, a car, a truck, and a van.

M.   Households Replacing or Disposing of Vehicles

The estimates imply that both one- and two-vehicle households with more vehicles than drivers are more likely to replace than add an additional vehicle. This coefficient is significant for two-vehicle households. For both one- and two-vehicle households, the alternative-dispose constant for households with a member over 60 years old is, as expected, positive and significant. This shows that older people are more likely to dispose of their vehicles.

N.   Other Vehicle Type Effects

The coefficient associated with replacing a station wagon with a van has an expected positive sign for both one- and two-vehicle households; that is, people are more likely to replace a station wagon with a van. Also, for both one- and two-vehicle households, the alternative-replace constant for households in which the held vehicle's type is the same as the *SP* vehicle's type, is positive and significant. This implies that many households decide to replace their old vehicle with a new vehicle of the same type.

O.   Alternative-Replace Constant for Replacing a Cheaper Vehicle

This variable is only applicable for two-vehicle households. When a household decides to replace one of their held vehicles, the one that is more likely to be replaced is not necessarily the older one, but the one which has lower market value. The results support this idea through the positive and significant coefficient for "Alternative-replace constant · Lower value vehicle".

P.   Electric Vehicle Interactions with Geographic Variables

For two-vehicle households, the fuel-type electric (EV) dummy variable interacts with three geographic dummy variables: Los Angeles metropolitan area; San Francisco, Oakland, and San Jose; and Northern California excluding San Francisco, Oakland, and San Jose. All three coefficients are negative. The coefficient for EV fuel-type interacting with Los Angeles has the largest negative value, and is the only significant one. This implies that households in the Los Angeles Metropolitan Area are less inclined to purchase EV's than households in other urban areas in California, *ceteris paribus*. This is consistent with the hypothesis that those choosing to live in the Los Angeles area have demonstrated a higher tolerance for air pollution.

VII.   FORECASTS

Although the models' coefficients can be used to see how households trade off various vehicle characteristics, these tradeoffs cannot be easily translated into market demand estimates for specific vehicles. This section describes some simple forecasting exercises which use the models specified in the previous section to produce market demand forecasts for some specific future scenarios.

A.   Forecasting Scenarios

The main source of the data for these scenarios is the 1993/1994 Draft Energy Analysis Report from the California Energy Commission (February, 1994, P300-94-002). The report provides data on price, operating costs, shoulder room, luggage space, horsepower, and range for 36 body type/size classes of vehicles expected to be available in 1998. Unfortunately, our model also requires information on acceleration time and top speed for these vehicles. To support our model estimation, this information was collected for all existing vehicles between 1978 and 1992. These data were then used to estimate regression models which were in turn used to predict acceleration and top speed for each vehicle type/size class in 1998.

These models had a very high goodness-of-fit: the adjusted R^2 values for acceleration and top speed are .98 and .96 respectively. One problem with this procedure is that it assumes that the relationship between acceleration, top speed, vehicle class, horsepower, efficiency, shoulder room, and luggage space is the same for each fuel type. Although this is probably true for gasoline, methanol, and *CNG*, it may not be true for *EV*s. Nevertheless, this method appears to give reasonable values for *EV*s as well.

The prices for Electric Vehicles (*EV*s) were set at $10,000 higher than a comparable gasoline vehicle. These numbers were suggested in discussions with Southern California Edison (*SCE*) and California Energy Commission (*CEC*) staff. All prices are in 1993 dollars. Values are given for horsepower in each class, although they are not currently being used in the choice models. If any of the 14 body type/size classes are missing for a particular fuel type, then that type/size class was assumed to not be available for that fuel type in 1998. Operating cost is cents/mile, and acceleration is seconds needed to reach 30 miles per hour.

Gasoline Vehicles

The range for all gasoline vehicles is assumed to be 400 miles, the price of gasoline $1.42 per gallon, and it was assumed to take 7 minutes to refuel an empty fuel tank. A fuel availability index of 1.0 (gasoline available at all current stations) and a pollution index of .90 (indicating that 1998 gasoline vehicles are slightly cleaner than comparable 1994 models) were used. The gasoline vehicle details for the scenario are described in Table 5.

Methanol

Scenario data for methanol vehicles is detailed in Table 6. The fuel availability index for methanol is .10 and the pollution index

Table 5. Forecast Scenario for Gasoline Vehicles

Class Code	Vehicle Class	Price	MPG	Horse-power	Accel. Time	Top Speed	Oper. Cost
1	Car-Mini	12908	33	109	3.2	124	4.35
2	Car-Subcompact	12162	30	103	3.8	114	4.78
3	Car-Compact	16684	25	131	3.2	125	5.75
4	Car-Midsize	18742	23	155	3.0	129	6.12
5	Car-Large	20322	21	173	3.3	124	6.79
6	Car-Luxury	36536	20	206	2.8	133	7.24
7	Car-Sport	17105	23	159	2.7	136	6.26
8	Pickup-Compact	13430	21	132	3.3	124	6.67
9	Pickup-Standard	17068	15	185	3.5	120	9.42
10	Van-Compact	19699	20	148	3.2	125	7.17
11	Van-Standard	17433	15	182	3.8	113	9.52
12	Sport Utility-Compact	21417	19	161	3.1	127	7.65
13	Sport Utility-Standard	23266	14	205	3.5	118	10.27
14	Sport Utility-Mini	14377	26	87	4.4	100	5.43

Table 6. Forecast Scenario for Methanol Vehicles

Class Code	Vehicle Class	Price	MPG	Horse-power	Accel. Time	Top Speed	Range	Oper. Cost
15	Car-Subcompact	12350	32	109	3.7	115	244	3.81
16	Car-Compact	16872	26	139	3.1	128	242	4.58
17	Car-Midsize	18965	25	164	2.9	132	267	4.87
18	Car-Large	20585	22	183	3.1	126	261	5.40
19	Car-Luxury	36589	21	218	2.7	135	264	5.76
20	Pickup-Compact	13653	23	140	3.1	127	262	5.31
21	Pickup-Standard	17329	16	196	3.3	123	300	7.50
22	Van-Standard	17694	16	193	3.7	116	300	7.58

Table 7. Forecast Scenario for CNG Vehicles

Class Code	Vehicle Class	Price	MPG	Horse-power	Accel. Time	Top Speed	Range	Oper. Cost
23	Car-Subcompact	14405	30	91	4.2	106	180	3.30
24	Car-Compact	18926	25	119	3.6	119	180	3.98
25	Car-Midsize	20984	24	143	3.3	124	180	4.23
26	Car-Large	22367	21	159	3.6	119	180	4.69
27	Car-Luxury	19831	15	170	2.7	138	180	6.51
28	Pickup-Compact	22489	21	145	2.8	135	180	4.85
29	Pickup-Standard	20200	15	167	3.8	114	180	6.58
30	Sport Utility-Standard	20740	14	160	4.2	105	160	7.01

118

is .70. The fuel price is $1.21 per gallon, and it takes 7 minutes to refuel an empty fuel tank. All vehicles have "flex-fuel" capability, but the range and operating costs in the table assume M85 operation.

Compressed Natural Gas (CNG)

Scenario data for *CNG* vehicles are in Table 7. The service station fuel availability index for *CNG* is .10 and the pollution index is .30. The fuel price is assumed to be equivalent to $1.00 per gallon, and it takes 7 minutes to refuel an empty fuel tank. All vehicles are assumed to be dedicated, except for Vehicle Class 30 which is dual fuel. Home refueling is assumed to be available for those households with natural gas service.

Electric Vehicles

Finally, scenario data for electric vehicles is given in Table 8. The service station fuel availability index for *EV*s is .10 and the tailpipe pollution index is 0.00. The operating costs are calculated by adding 7 cents per mile to the operating costs given in the CEC fuels report (which are also consistent with the figures provided in SCE Report Number U 338-E on "Emissions Reductions"). The 7 cents per mile figure accounts for battery replacement costing $2,000 every 3 years and driving 10,000 miles per year. All vehicles are assumed to be dedicated *EV*s, and home recharging is available for all households. It takes 4 hours to recharge a discharged *EV* at home.

B.   Forecast Results

Forecasts were computed using only those households in our sample that intended to purchase a new vehicle as part of their next transaction. The choice models give transaction probabilities for the households, where each choice alternative involves either an addition or a replacement transaction in which one of the 36 vehicles from the scenario tables is purchased. For a given sample household, these probabilities can be intrepreted as the predicted

Table 8. Forecast Scenario for Electric Vehicles

Class Code	Vehicle Class	Price	MPG	Horse-power	Accel. Time	Top Speed	Range	Oper. Cost
31	Car-Mini	22908	168	45	5.2	78	80	8.57
32	Car-Subcompact	22162	106	60	5.1	78	100	9.48
33	Car-Compact	26684	71	75	5.1	79	100	10.71
34	Car-Sport	27105	86	100	4.4	92	100	10.06
35	Pickup-Compact	23430	66	62	5.7	66	120	10.98
36	Van-Compact	29699	49	70	5.8	64	120	12.40

proportions associated with the much larger group of households in the general population that are observationally identical to the "representative" sample household. The sampling weights are used to estimate the number of these observationally identical households, so that forecasts for the entire population may be derived by multiplying the choice probabilities by the sample weights.

The one-vehicle household model predicts choice probabilities for 73 discrete alternatives: replacing the existing vehicle with one of the 36 hypothetical vehicles (described in the scenario tables), adding one of the 36 hypothetical vehicles, and disposing of the current vehicle. The two-vehicle household model predicts choice probabilities for 110 alternatives: replacing the existing first vehicle with one of the 36 hypothetical vehicles, replacing the second, adding one of the 36 hypothetical vehicles, disposing of the first existing vehicle, and disposing of the second vehicle.

The transaction models do not predict the timing of the transaction, just the type of transaction. We give forecasts only for those households (605 one-vehicle and 691 two-vehicle, representing 46 and 52 percent of all one and two-vehicle households, respectively) who indicated that their next vehicle transaction would involve purchasing a new vehicle. Since this choice rules out disposing of a vehicle and not purchasing a new one, we only produce forecasts for the alternatives that include a new vehicle purchase. The resulting forecasts can be interpreted as the results of 4-5 years of new car purchasing with only the 36 hypothetical vehicle types available.

Since we have not carefully analyzed the changes in the sampling weights caused by excluding households with missing data, we only present forecasts in terms of purchase shares. These shares should be more reliable than the underlying forecasts of absolute numbers of vehicle sales.

All of the forecasts are given in terms of 90 percent confidence bands. These bands incorporate the uncertainty in the parameter estimates from the two models. The true purchase shares should fall inside these bands 90 percent of the time if the entire survey and estimation process were independently replicated many times.

Table 9.   Combined Household Forecast Shares by Transaction

Transaction Type	Fuel Type	Lower Bound	Median	Upper Bound
Replace	Gasoline	43.2	49.2	55.2
	Methanol	11.3	15.1	18.5
	CNG	11.2	13.8	16.5
	Electric	2.2	2.9	3.5
Add	Gasoline	9.9	11.5	13.6
	Methanol	2.3	3.0	3.8
	CNG	2.6	3.3	3.9
	Electric	0.5	0.7	0.9

Table 10.   Combined Household Forecast Shares

Fuel Type	Lower Bound	Median	Upper Bound
Gasoline	53.2	60.9	68.1
Methanol	13.6	18.3	22.3
CNG	13.8	17.2	20.4
Electric	2.6	3.6	4.4

Tables 9 and 10 give purchase shares for one and two-vehicle households. These are given by transaction type (replace or add) and also combined. The "median" shares do not always add up to 100 percent because of rounding errors and the fact that the confidence bands are not perfectly symmetric.

C.   Sensitivity Analysis

Since the forecasting models are quite complex, it is difficult to judge the sensitivity of the forecasts to changes in key exogenous variables. To help understand these sensitivities, we present the results of four different changes from the baseline scenario.

One problem with the pollution variable is that it doesn't represent a private cost to any of the respondents, so they may choose a low-pollution hypothetical vehicle to indicate a preference for public policies designed to reduce pollution. To produce an estimate of the upper bound for this effect, we set the

Table 11.   Change in Purchase Share by Fuel Type

Change from Base Scenario	Electric	CNG	Methanol	Gasoline
No Pollution	-0.8	-2.2	-0.1	3.1
EV Price Reduced by $10,000	1.4	-0.3	-0.2	-0.9
EV operating cost increased 25%	-0.6	0.1	0.1	0.4
EV range increased 25%	0.4	-0.1	-0.1	-0.2

pollution level for all vehicles equal to .9 and run the forecasts again. The results are given in the first row of the following table. We also consider the effects of changing EV purchase price, operating costs, and range.

Not surprisingly, the main effect of removing the pollution variable is to reduce the demand for electric vehicles by almost 25 percent. Neutralizing this demand reduction would require reducing EV purchase prices by approximately $6,000 and/or increasing EV range substantially more than 25 percent. The sensitivity results broadly show that changing EV vehicle characteristics has a proportionately larger effect on CNG vehicle demand. This is as expected since CNG vehicles also have limited range and refueling options.

Although all of the scenarios represented in Table 11 still show EV purchase shares meeting the 1998 California 2 percent mandate, the results also show the difficulty of increasing EV penetration much past 5 percent. Even if EV purchase price and range are substantially improved, significant market penetration will require the availability of EVs in a broader range of body types than those given in Table 8.

The confidence bands for the changes in the above table are also shifted by the same amount. Due to the highly non-linear nature of the forecasting models, it is inadvisable to extrapolate these sensitivity results beyond the figures given in Table 11.

VIII.   CONCLUSIONS

The modeling system described in this paper is capable of analyzing most of the proposed policies for stimulating the demand for alternative-fuel vehicles. The system can also be used by vehicle manufacturers to help gauge the demand for various types and configurations of alternative-fuel vehicles. This preliminary work suggests that consumers' responses to our hypothetical vehicle choice experiments are realistic, but the only proof of this assertion will come when alternative-fuel vehicles similar to these hypothetical vehicles are actually offered in the marketplace.

The model forecasts the demand for future vehicles conditioned on the current holdings of the household. The estimation results show that high-income households or households currently holding luxury vehicles are likely to buy high-priced vehicles, households with children are more sensitive to air pollution than households without children, vehicle range is a very important concern to households when they buy alternative-fuel vehicles, acceleration time is important only for high income households; refueling time seems not too important since most alternative-fuel vehicles can either refuel at home or use gasoline, households with more cars than drivers are more likely to replace their held vehicles, households with more drivers than cars are likely to add a vehicle, households with a child of age 15 or 16 are also likely to add a vehicle, and households with one member's age over 60 are more likely to scrap a vehicle.

Based on this model, we have computed forecasts for households who intend to purchase new vehicles. Median forecast shares for gasoline, methanol, *CNG*, and electric vehicles are 60.9, 18.3, 17.2, and 3.6 percent. These forecast electric vehicle shares are slightly higher than those found in previous work discussed in Section II, but each of these studies made different assumptions about vehicle technology. If the scenarios presented in Tables 5-8 are accurate predictions of the vehicles offered in 1998, then manufacturers will be able to sell enough electric and other alternative-fuel vehicles to meet the current 1998 California mandates.

The models used in this paper can only be sensitive to features of new vehicles that were included in the questionnaire. Therefore we are unable to include other potentially important vehicle attributes such as reliability and maintenance costs (including battery replacement) which may be different from existing gasoline vehicles. Data currently being collected as part of a follow-up survey of the same households will allow us to assess the importance of these other attributes.

The main reason for promoting alternative-fuel vehicles is to reduce urban air pollution. A full evaluation of any policy promoting alternative-fuel vehicles for reducing pollution must also consider other competing policies such as promoting mass transit use and policies designed to reduce the use of conventional vehicles. This full analysis is beyond the scope of our current efforts, although we hope to extend our model system in the future to make it more useful for evaluating a broader range of pollution and congestion-reducing policies.

APPENDIX: VEHICLE CHOICE SURVEY QUESTION

Suppose that you were considering purchasing a vehicle and the following three vehicles were available: (assume that gasoline costs $1.20 per gallon)

	Vehicle A	Vehicle B	Vehicle C
Fuel Type	Electric Runs on electricity only.	Natural Gas (CNG) Runs on CNG only.	Methanol Can also run on gasoline.
Vehicle Range	80 miles	120 miles on CNG	300 miles on methanol
Purchase Price	$21,000 (includes home charge unit)	$19,000 (includes home refueling unit)	$23,000
Home Refueling Time	8 hrs for full charge (80 miles)	2 hrs to fill empty tank (120 miles)	Not Available
Home Refueling Fuel Cost	2 cents per mile (50 MPG gasoline equiv.) for recharging between 6 pm and 10 am 10 cents per mile (10 MPG gasoline equiv.) for recharging between 10 am and 6 pm	4 cents per mile (25 MPG gasoline equiv.)	

(continued)

Appendix (Continued)

	Vehicle A	Vehicle B	Vehicle C
Service Station Refueling Time	10 min. for full charge (80 mi.)	10 min. to fill empty CNG tank (120 mi.)	6 min. to fill empty tank (300 mi.)
Service Station Fuel Cost	10 cents per mile (10 MPG gasoline equiv.)	4 cents per mile (25 MPG gasoline equiv.)	4 cents per mile (25 MPG gasoline equiv.)
Service Station Availability	1 recharge station for every 10 gasoline stations	1 CNG station for every 10 gasoline stations	Gasoline available at current stations
Acceleration Time to 30 mph	6 seconds	2.5 seconds	4 seconds
Top Speed	65 miles per hour	80 miles per hour	80 miles per hour
Tailpipe Emissions	"Zero" tailpipe emissions	25% of new 1993 gasoline car emissions when run on CNG	Like new 1993 gasoline cars when run on methanol
Vehicle Size	Like a compact car	Like a sub-compact car	Like a mid-size car
Body Types	Car or Truck	Car or Van	Car or Truck
Luggage Space	Like a comparable gasoline vehicle	Like a comparable gasoline vehicle	Like a comparable gasoline vehicle

1. Given these choices, which vehicle would you purchase? (please circle one choice)

   (1) Vehicle "A" (car)
   (2) Vehicle "A" (truck)
   (3) Vehicle "B" (car)
   (4) Vehicle "B" (van)
   (5) Vehicle "C" (car)
   (6) Vehicle "C" (truck)

2. Would this vehicle most likely be purchased as a replacement vehicle for your household, or as an additional vehicle?

   (1) Replacement   (2) Additional

3. If you choose "Replacement" in Question 2, please cross off the household vehicle that would be replaced from the following list:

   (1) 1990 Ford Bronco   (2) 1989 Toyota Camry

ACKNOWLEDGMENTS

Funding for the work reported in this paper has been provided by the Southern California Edison Co. and Pacific Gas and Electric Co. In addition to our project managers—Ernest Morales and Richard Rice (Southern California Edison Co.) and Dan Fitzgerald (Pacific Gas and Electric Co.)—the authors wish to thank their colleagues—Ryuichi Kitamura, Mark Bradley, Stuart Hardy, Seyoung Kim, Jane Torous, Soheila Crane and Camilla Kazimi—who have all contributed enormously to the work described in this paper. In addition, Gary Occhiuzzo, Mike Jaske, and Tim Tutt of the California Energy Commission, Debbie Brodt of Southern California Edison, and Lisa Cooper of Pacific Gas and Electric have worked diligently on behalf of the project. None of these kind people or their organizations are responsible for any errors or for the specific views expressed here.

REFERENCES

Beggs, S., Cardell, S., & Hausman, J. (1981). Assessing the potential demand for electric cars. *Journal of Econometrics, 16,* 1-19.

Ben-Akiva, M., & Morikawa, T. (1990). Estimation of travel demand models from multiple data sources. In Masaki Koshi (Ed.), *Transportation and traffic theory : Proceedings of the eleventh international symposium on transportation and traffic theory.* New York: Elsevier.

Bradley, M., & Daly, A. (1993, July). *Estimation of logit choice models using information from both stated preferences and revealed preferences.* Discussion paper for the Duke International Symposium on Choice Modeling and Behavior.

Bunch, D.S., Bradley, M., Golob, T.F., Kitamura, R., & Occhiuzzo, G.P. (1993). Demand for alternative-fuel vehicles in California: A discrete-choice stated preference pilot project. *Transportation Research, 27A,* 237-253.

Calfee, J.E. (1985). Estimating the demand for electric automobiles using fully disaggregated probabilistic choice analysis. *Transportation Research, 19B,* 287-302.

Crow, R., & Ratchford, B. (1977). *Classical qualitative choice and new goods: An application to electric automobiles.* Unpublished paper, Electric Power Research Institute, Palo Alto, California.

Dickson, E., & Walton, B. (1977). *A scenario of battery/electric vehicle market evaluation.* Unpublished Stanford Research Institute Report, SRI, Menlo Park, CA.

Efron, B., & Tibshirani, R. (1993). *An introduction to the bootstrap.* New York: Chapman and Hall.

Fowkes, T., & Wardman, M. (1988). The design of stated preference travel choice experiments, with special reference to inter-personal taste variations. *Journal of Transport Economics and Policy, 22,* 27-44.

Golob, T.F., Bunch, D.S. & Brownstone, D. (1996). A vehicle usage forecasting model based on revealed and stated vehicle type choice and utilization data. *Journal of Transport Economics and Policy,* (in press).

Golob, T.F., Brownstone, D., Bunch, D.S., & Kitamura, R. (1995, August). *Forecasting electric vehicle ownership and use in the California South Coast air basin.* Draft final report submitted to the Southern California Edison Company.

Hausman, J., & McFadden, D. (1984). Specification tests for the multinomial logit model. *Econometrica, 52,* 1219-1240.

Hensher, D.A. (1982). Functional measurements, individual preferences and discrete choice modeling: Theory and application. *Journal of Econometric Psychology, 2,* 323-335.

Hensher, D.A., Smith, N.C., Milthorpe, N.W., & Barnard, P.O. (1992). *Dimensions of automobile demand.* Amsterdam: Elsevier.

Hensher, D.A., Barnard, P.O., & Truong, T.P. (1988). The role of stated preference methods in studies of travel choice. *Journal of Transport Economics and Policy, 22,* 45-70 .

Hensher, D.A. (1994). Stated preference analysis of travel choices: The state of practice. *Transportation, 21,* 107-133.

Hill, M. (1992). *The panel study of income dynamics: A users guide.* Newberry Park, CA: Sage Publications.

Karfisi, E., Upton, C., & Agnew, C. (1978). *The impact of electric passenger automobiles on utility system loads, 1985-2000.* Report EA-623 to Electric Power Research Institute, research project 751-1.

Kazimi, C. (1995). *A microsimulation model for evaluating the environmental impact of alternative-fuel vehicles.* Unpublished Ph.D. dissertation, Department of Economics, University of California, Irvine.

Kroes, E.P., & Sheldon, R.J. (1988). Stated preference methods: An introduction. *Journal of Transport Economics and Policy, 22,* 11-26.

Lave, C., & Train, K. (1979). A disaggregate model of auto-type choice. *Transportation Research, 13A,* 1-9.

Louviere, J. (1988). Conjoint analysis modeling of stated preferences: A review of theory, methods, recent developments and external validity. *Journal of Transport Economics and Policy, 22*, 93-120.

Morikawa, T. (1994). Estimation of discrete choice models from serially correlated RP and SP data. *Transportation, 21*, 185-165.

SRI. (1978, May). *Electric Vehicle News.*

Train, K. (1980a). The potential demand for electric vehicles. *Transportation Research, 14A*, 405-414.

Train, K. (1980b). A structured logit model of auto ownership and mode choice. *Review of Economic Studies, XLVII*, 357-370.

Train, K. (1986). *Qualitative choice analysis: Econometrics and an application to automobile demand.* Cambridge, MA: MIT Press.

Wardman, M. (1988). A Comparison of revealed preference and stated preference models of travel behaviour. *Journal of Transport Economics and Policy, 22*, 71-92.

Wharton Econometric Forecasting Associates, Inc. (1977). *An analysis of the automobile market: Modeling the long-run determinants of the demand for automobiles* (Vols. 1-3). Prepared for the U.S. Department of Transportation, Transportation Systems Center, Cambridge, MA.

AN ECONOMIC ANALYSIS OF TRUCKER'S INCENTIVE TO OVERLOAD AS AFFECTED BY THE JUDICIAL SYSTEM

Eric L. Jessup

ABSTRACT

The primary objective of this paper was to investigate the economic incentive to overload trucks above the legal weight limit and provide a case study evaluating the effectiveness of Washington's fine system in deterring the economic incentive or recapturing the financial damage to roads and highways, through the court and legal process. A conceptual model of trucker's incentive to overload was developed and the relationship between that incentive and the effectiveness of the judicial system was then empirically investigated. This was accomplished through interviews with weight

Research in Transportation Economics, Volume 4, pages 131-159.

enforcement officials and court personnel in addition to a detailed examination of over 8,000 overweight citations from nine counties between September 1991 and August 1992. The punitive rate, evaluated through the average percent of original fine paid, on contested cases for the state was 56.3 percent. For cases that were contested and found guilty, the punitive rate was only 63 percent, indicating that 37 percent of potential revenue from this source is being lost in the court system. The punitive rate on all cases did not vary much across different counties. However, the average percent of original fine paid on contested cases was much higher for smaller counties and counties without port of entries, suggesting that judges in smaller counties regard overweight violations a more serious offense than judges from larger counties. These results can be used to provide a better understanding of firm's decision to overload and inform lawmakers and judges about the purpose and role of the fee and fine system in controlling overweight violations and financial recovery of road damage.

I. INTRODUCTION

The highway/road system is a significant investment in sustaining the regional and national economy. However, the current road and highway system is experiencing accelerated deterioration. One of the causes of accelerated deterioration is heavily loaded trucks, whether operating legally (with a permit) or illegally.

In research by the Transportation Research Board (TRB), it was concluded that states should examine their current weight enforcement practices. "The effort of identification of overloaded vehicles is not justified if the judicial system does not handle offenders effectively." Casavant recommends that "...research into the effectiveness of the court system...might be useful" for the state of Washington (Casavant, 1991a).

Several factors influence the economic incentive to load trucks above the legal weight limit (Casavant, 1991b). The case study provided in this analysis includes factors such as types of responses to citations, fine reductions for contested cases, percentage of original fine collected by the state, and allocation of fines collected by the state. This information may help determine which variables have the largest influence on the firm's decision to overload and increase states' awareness of the importance of a fine system in attaining the funds needed to repair pavement damage caused by overweight trucks. Findings could ultimately aid transportation officials in arriving at a means to decrease the rate of pavement deterioration or procure the funds required to repair the damages caused by illegally overloaded trucks, and to enforce this fine and fee system.

The purpose of this study is to investigate the firm's decision to overload trucks and determine how the court system and judicial process influences that decision through deterrence and recapturing the financial damage to pavements caused by overloaded trucks. Evaluation of Washington's fee and fine system is then provided as a case study, examining its effectiveness and influence on overloading activity.

II. ECONOMIC RATIONALE FOR TRUCK OVERLOADING

The decision to overload trucks is based on the expectation of economic gain. Decreased transportation cost per unit is weighed against the expected cost or penalty associated with overloading. However, many factors influence the difference between transportation cost savings and the penalty from overloading, and therefore the number of overweight trucks on roads and highways, including the fee/fine system, courts (e.g., judges' decisions and fine collection processes), and the capture rate or numbers of trucks being apprehended and fined. The fee/fine system dictates the dollar amount attached to overweight permits and assigns a schedule of fines for truck loads in excess of legal weight limits. If permit fees and overload fines are established too low, the net benefit to the shipper from overloading becomes greater and the number of overloaded trucks increase. A similar relationship exists between the courts and the number of overloaded trucks on the states highways. If judges routinely dismiss or reduce fines to a fraction of the original amount, the incentive to overload trucks increases. And if enforcement authorities are not effective capturing overweight vehicles and providing the risk of capture to overloaded truck operators, overloading activity will increase regardless of the fee/fine system and the courts effectiveness.

The type of commodity being transported also influences the decision to overload. Some commodities, because of their physical and spacial attributes, are not capable of producing weights in excess of legal truck weight limits. Typically, natural resource and agricultural commodities with dense weight characteristics are likely candidates for truck overloading.

III. THEORETICAL MODEL

Theoretically, the willingness to overload is a function of decreased per unit cost (economic benefits) versus the fee that must be paid to legally overload and/or the perception of risk associated with being "captured" and fined. When the economic benefit of overloading exceeds the costs (fees/fines), overloading will occur. However, as long as the fee or net fine sufficiently recaptures the deterioration to roads and highways, society benefits. Loss to society occurs when the damage to roads exceeds the revenue from fees and fines. Notice the goal is not to minimize road damage because some overloads, when paid for by truckers, do contribute a positive economic impact to the economy and society. Thus, the aim is to balance the amount of overloading with the recapture of damage. However, integral to the recapture process is the courts' effectiveness in fine enforcement (punitive rate).

The action of interest here is the occurrence of overweight vehicles. The incentive to overload is an economic one which can be captured through the evaluation of the firm. If we consider the party responsible for deciding truck load size to be a profit maximizing firm, the following relationship can be used to represent the firm's objective function.

$$Max \ \pi = PQ - C - C(Q) + \lambda_1(L - Q) + \lambda_2(T - Q) \quad (1)$$

where:

π = profit per truckload
P = price per unit transported
Q = quantity per truckload
C = fixed cost per truckload
$C(Q)$ = variable cost per truckload
L = legal weight limit per truckload
T = physical truck weight capacity per truckload

Assuming perfect competition, the firm maximizes profit through their choice of Q, subject to two constraints on the legal and physical truck capacity. Profit is maximized by subtracting both fixed (C) and variable costs $(C(Q))$ from total revenue per truckload (PQ). Variable cost is a function of the quantity chosen per truckload and, when divided by Q, is expected to decrease as the quantity per truckload increases. Average fixed cost will also decline as the quantity per truckload increases, resulting in decreasing average total cost, as depicted in Figure 1. The reason for this relationship is because variable and fixed cost are spread across more units, resulting in lower average total cost per unit as the number of units per truckload increases. Then, assuming the neoclassical assumptions about the firm's behavior hold, we should be able to determine the level of Q which maximizes the firm's objective function by taking the first order conditions and solving for Q.

First Order Conditions:

$$\frac{\partial \pi}{\partial Q} = P - C'(Q) - \lambda_1 - \lambda_2 \qquad (2)$$

Equation 2 represents the change in profit associated with a change in the quantity per truckload as indicated by the per unit price (P), minus the per unit variable cost and the shadow prices associated with the two constraints. The coefficients associated with λ_1 and λ_2 represent the marginal addition to profit

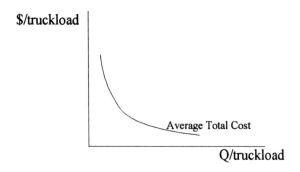

Figure 1. Relationship Between Average Total Costs
and Quantity Shipped per Truckload

associated with relaxing each constraint one unit. Equations 3 and
4 symbolize these two constraints.

$$\frac{\partial \pi}{\partial \lambda_1} = L - Q = 0 \qquad (3)$$

$$\frac{\partial \pi}{\partial \lambda_2} = T - Q = 0 \qquad (4)$$

Solving for the choice variable (Q), in this situation, creates a
difficulty because other factors influence "Q." The process of
choosing the quantity per truck load is not an independent event,
but rather a function of several random variables. Therefore, the
function Q can be generally written as:

$$Q = f(\alpha, \gamma, \mu,) \qquad (5)$$

where:

α = capture rate of overweight trucks
γ = punitive rate (proportion of fine paid for overweight
    violations)
μ = other influences related to the commodity (e.g. bulkiness
    and fragility of commodity).

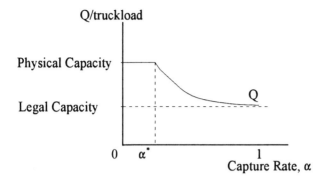

Figure 2. Relationship Between the Capture Rate
and Quantity per Truckload

The exact specification of this function is unknown. However, we can identify certain relationships expected between the two variables α and γ and the quantity chosen per truckload. The functional relationship between the capture rate of overweight vehicles (α) and the quantity chosen (Q) is not a continuously smooth function, as illustrated in Figure 2. The capture rate ranges from zero to one depending on, among other factors, the enforcement effort, location, truck type and time of day. At low capture rates (say zero), truckers have the incentive to maximize the payload, and thus profits, by loading trucks to their physical capacity. At some point (α^*), as the capture rate increases, the quantity per truckload begins decreasing as a result of the increasing risk associated with overloading. As the capture rate approaches 100 percent, Q asymptotically approaches the legal truck weight limit. A very similar relationship exists with respect to the punitive rate (γ). If truckers anticipate extremely lenient judges who either dismiss fines completely or drastically reduce them to a fraction of the original amount, then the incentive to load trucks to their maximum payload exists. However, as the proportion of fine paid increases (γ), the quantity per truckload decreases to the legal truck capacity. This relationship assumes that the physical truck capacity always exceeds the legal truck weight limit which may not necessarily be the case for some commodities and products. However, for those commodities which possess the physical attributes conducive to truck overloading, the physical truck capacity will exceed the legal weight capacity. The primary interest of this analysis is the investigation of vehicle overloading, since trucks operating at or below the legal weight limit are not a problem.

The process of choosing the quantity per truckload, and thus the decision to overload or not and to what degree, depends largely upon the random variables α and γ. Therefore, the function Q can be represented as a combination of two conditional probabilities representing the random events of being captured and the proportion of fine paid, given being captured. Specifically, the choice of Q can be written as follows:

$EQ = f(Prob.\ of\ capture\ |\ being\ overloaded,$

(6)

$Proportion\ of\ fine\ paid\ |\ being\ overloaded\ |\ being\ captured)$

The expectation of the function Q is a function of two conditional events: (1) the probability of being captured, given that the truck is overloaded, and (2) the proportion of fine paid, given that the truck is both overloaded and captured.

Empirical estimates of the capture rate (α) of between 20 percent and 27 percent of overloaded truck traffic have been recently reported in the state of Washington (Jessup & Casavant, 1995). However, few, if any, investigations of the effectiveness of the court and legal system in constraining trucker's operations have been conducted. The focus of this analysis is estimating this punitive rate (γ) in equation 5. There is some difficulty in arriving at estimates of capture and punitive rates which apply universally since these rates vary with location and time. However, the following case study provides estimates from nine counties within the state of Washington, allowing an initial understanding of the effectiveness of the court and legal process and its impact on overloading activity.

IV. WASHINGTON'S FEE/FINE SYSTEM: A CASE STUDY

To control or recapture pavement damage caused by overloaded trucks (and to promote safety), Washington has a weight enforcement system consisting of fees (permits) and fines (penalties). This system was designed to control the economic incentive to overload and/or to recover the road damage associated with the extra weight. The state's fee and fine system serves to both deter overloading and provide financial recovery from resultant damage.

Washington's fee and fine structure is implemented via a two-step process: (1) Enforcement of weight regulations by designated agencies (capture rate) and (2) the legal/court process and actions (punitive rate). Those involved in the first step of the process include Washington State Patrol (WSP), sheriff's offices, and other commercial vehicle enforcement officers (CVEOs), often employed by City Public Works departments. The District Courts (county courts) are responsible for the second step, the adjudication process, which is the focus of this study. An overweight violation is categorized as a traffic infraction and the fine associated with it can either be paid or contested in a District Court.

Funds from fines collected through paid and contested cases are divided between the state of Washington and the local district court. By statute, the overall revenue split for moving violations is 57/43 percent (local/state)(Revised Code of Washington 3.62). District Courts deposit these funds into several different accounts such as the current expense account (including road maintenance) and crime victims account. All funds allocated to the state are deposited into the Public Safety and Education Account (PSEA) and appropriated by the Legislature for programs ranging from traffic safety and wildlife to judicial education and crime victims compensation. The PSEA does not currently provide funding for road repair and construction. But, since they are part of the state's general revenue fund, the PSEA funds are effectively substitution for other funds (road construction) that would have had to be spent on these activities. Thus, the fines are effectively available to service general state needs including roads.

Nine Washington counties were chosen to be evaluated in this analysis:

1. Benton County
2. Clark County
3. Grays Harbor County
4. King County
5. Kittitas County
6. Pierce County
7. Skagit County
8. Spokane County
9. Walla Walla County

They were picked mainly because of their location and economic base. These include five counties with Ports of Entry (POEs) (permanent scale sites at state borders that normally operate 24 hours daily), one county in the far west, two in western Washington along I-5 and one in the middle of the state along I-90 (Figure 3). Additional characteristics such as major income base (logging, agricultural and heavy industrial) and population were also incorporated into county selection. The data for this study were obtained from overweight citations issued in Washington between September 1, 1991 and August 31, 1992 (For a full description of the data set see Barron et al., 1994). It was determined through phone calls to District Courts across the state that the only feasible means of tracing citations was through the use of citation numbers or names to whom the tickets were issued. Filing systems in District Courts were classified using defendants' names or ticket numbers. These numbers or names could be used to retrieve either the hard copies or computer data entries of the citations filed in the District Courts.

Citation numbers were obtained through the WSP Commercial Vehicle Enforcement Section (CVES) in Olympia. CVEOs answered the request with approximately 8,000 citation numbers. Two sheriff's departments also provided citation numbers.

The most efficient way to retrieve data from the citation numbers was from the Courts' DISCUS system (a system consisting of complete information on citations and their

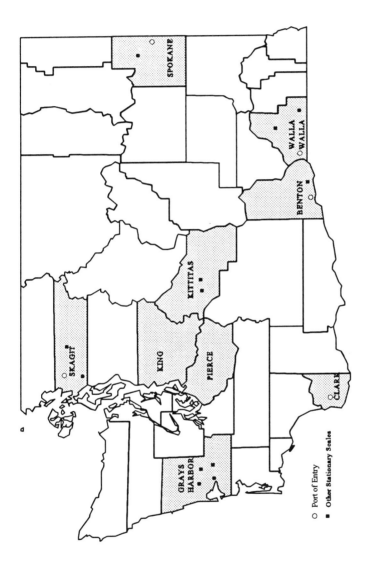

Figure 3. Location of Washington Counties Analyzed

○ Port of Entry

■ Other Stationary Scales

141

dispositions) accessed through a computer in Spokane District Court. In deciding sample size, a confidence level of 99 percent and an error (maximum difference between the sample mean and population mean that was acceptable for the 99 percent confidence level indicated) of $25.00 (on the difference between original fine and fine paid) were chosen. That means, for instance, that, with 99 percent confidence, the average difference between the average original fine and the average fine paid in a sample area will fall within $25.00 of the true average difference for that area. The formula was applied using a population standard deviation derived from the first 50 citations in each area; statistical sample sizes ranged from 10 to 63 and it was decided that 75 citations from each location would be analyzed. Citations for the sample population were selected through a random sampling procedure utilizing a table of 10,000 random digits. The sample sizes were statistically significant, irrespective of the number of citations issued in each county.

There were 8,193 citation numbers sent from WSP and 131 from two sheriff's offices. These numbers were from citations issued in the nine sample areas and accounted for 80 percent of the total weight violations (10,388) recorded by WSP in the entire state during the sample period. Therefore, the sample areas in this study are certainly representative of the whole state, not only because of their locations and sources of major income, but because of the number of citations issued in these areas relative to the total for the state.

V.   EMPIRICAL ANALYSIS

The courts' effectiveness (punitive rate) is influenced by location since district courts assume the responsibility of implementation. However, additional characteristics (variables) associated with overweight citations can provide useful insight and a more accurate depiction of the courts' effectiveness, especially when compared across different locations (counties) within the state. The empirical results in this section are divided into sub-analyses representing variables such as vehicle weight, fines, court location, defendant's address, violation magnitude and type of response. Collectively, these sub-analyses characterize the court's role and effectiveness in influencing and controlling overloading activity. These sub-analyses also provide a better evaluation of the punitive rate (γ) and how each variable influences that rate and the trucker's decision to overload.

A. Weight

The number of trucks cited for weight violations in Washington over the past five years suggest there is indeed an economic incentive to overload (Table 1). The violatión magnitudes on citations in this study also imply that there may be flaws in Washington's commercial vehicle weight enforcement/fine system. Numerous trucks were cited for being very heavy overweight. In Skagit County a citation was written for a truck that was overloaded by 110,800 pounds (Table 2). Maximum overloads in each county, which ranged from 13,500 to 110,800 pounds, are evidence that there are very heavy trucks traveling on Washington's roads and highways. The magnitude of overload did not vary closely with how rural or urban the counties were.

CVEOs across the state enforce weight limits through the use of permanent, portable and semi-portable scales. Data from citations indicate that CVEOs display little tolerance regarding

Table 1. Number of Citations Issued in Washington
for Commercial Vehicle Weight Violations
and Resultant Civil Assessments, 1988-1992

| | Violation Type | | | | |
Year	Axle	Gross	Bridge	Total	Assessments
1988	8,727	2,920	1,699	13,346	$2,523,806
1989	8,035	2,409	1,729	12,173	$2,436,380
1990	7,249	3,696	1,446	12,391	$2,492,478
1991	7,090	1,035	1,588	9,713	$2,468,178
1992	7,456	446	1,823	10,725	$3,154,126

Source: Washington State Patrol (1989-1993).

Table 2.   Average, Minimum and Maximum Excess Weights (lbs.)
For Each County

Court	Average Excess Weight	Minimum Excess Weight	Maximum Excess Weight
BENTON	3,355	1,100	15,400
CLARK	3,203	700	33,600
GRAYS HARBOR	2,755	200	13,500
KING	3,871	1,000	20,700
KITTITAS	2,700	1,400	13,500
PIERCE	3,084	300	15,200
SKAGIT	5,309	1,300	110,800
SPOKANE	4,823	1,200	19,200
WALLA WALLA	4,403	1,200	23,400
OVERALL	3,693	200	110,800

breaches on weight limits. Minimum overloads ranged from 200
to 1,400 pounds suggesting that even those trucks that are causing
relatively little additional damage to the roads are being cited when
apprehended.

B.   Fines

In this section, the percentages of original fines collected by
the local courts are examined as an estimate of the state's punitive
rate (γ). Weaknesses and strengths in the current fine system and
the influence on trucker's economic incentive to overload may
be identified by analyzing this rate according to factors such as
court location, violation magnitude, address of defendant and
response.

Original fines, as used in this study, are the fines imposed on
weight violations at the time the citation is issued. They are
perfectly correlated with the violation magnitude or weight. All
fines start at $104.00 (for a first-time violation) and increase as
excess weight increases, on a $0.03 per pound scale. Original fines
in this study ranged from $110.00 for 200 pounds overweight to
$3,428.00 for a 110,800 pound overload (Table 3). The overall
average original fine was $215.00, indicating the potential of
recapturing a significant amount of revenue ($215 times 10,725

Table 3. Average, Minimum and Maximum Original Fines and Fines Paid In Each County ($ values)

County	Avg. Orig. Fine	Avg. Fine Paid	Min. Orig. Fine	Min. Fine Paid	Max. Orig. Fine	Max. Fine Paid
BENTON	205	164	137	50	566	566
CLARK	202	172	125	0	1112	1112
GRAYS HARBOR	187	155	110	0	509	360
KING	220	190	134	0	725	626
KITTITAS	185	169	146	0	509	449
PIERCE	196	154	113	0	560	434
SKAGIT	262	232	143	0	3428	2384
SPOKANE	249	230	140	0	680	641
WALLA WALLA	235	143	140	0	806	314
OVERALL	215	179	110	0	3428	2384

146   ERIC L. JESSUP

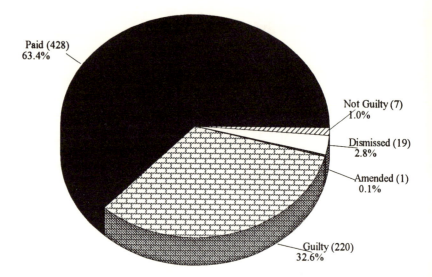

Figure 4. Case Dispositions on Overweight Violations
in Washington, 1991-1992

equals $2.3 million) for potential road repair/reconstruction, provided the defendants are (found) guilty.

Original fines can either be paid or contested in a District Court. There are three possible dispositions of a contested traffic infraction: Guilty, Not Guilty, and Dismissed (not guilty). The law reads that a person to whom a traffic infraction has been issued has 15 working days to respond; however, many courts allow 60 to 90 days for a response. If the defendant does not respond within that specified time, the case is charged, by the courts, as guilty. Fines associated with not guilty and dismissed cases are usually dropped or drastically reduced. As will be shown, fines on guilty charges are also frequently reduced, although to a lesser degree than not guilty and dismissed cases.

Paid cases (uncontested) were the most prevalent, accounting for 63 percent of the sample population (Figure 4). Of the thirty-seven percent that contested the citation, thirty-three percent of the defendants were found guilty, three percent of the cases were dismissed, one percent was not guilty, and one case was amended (from "over legal weight" to "no valid tonnage displayed"). Dispositions of citations included in this study are discussed further in a succeeding section.

Court Location

The punitive rate (γ), as estimated through the percentage of the original fine paid, in each county varied from 61 percent in Walla Walla County to 92 percent in Spokane County for all cases. Counties with POEs may place more emphasis on overweight violations since weight enforcement occurs 24 hours per day, seven days a week at POEs, thereby increasing the potential number of tickets. A further hypothesis could be drawn that judges in counties with smaller populations tended to reduce fines to a greater extent than the larger metropolitan courts. Although some single court data may support the above assumptions, aggregated analysis negated both hypotheses (Table 4). When considering all cases, there was a 3.4 percentage point difference found in the punitive rate in counties with POEs (81.4 percent) and in counties without POEs (84.8 percent). There was also little difference between the punitive rate (on all cases) in those counties with populations of less than 85,000 (81.8 percent) and the larger counties (83.8 percent). In fact, the counties with the lowest and the highest punitive rates both had populations of less than 85,000.

The punitive rate in contested cases was lower than those for all cases and ranged from 45 percent in Benton County to 82 percent in Skagit County. In the smaller counties (Grays Harbor, Kittitas, Skagit, and Walla Walla), an average of 66.9 percent of original fines were paid on contested cases found guilty. The judges in larger counties were more apt to lower fines on guilty cases; the punitive rate in counties with populations over 100,000 was an average of 58.3 percent. A similar case occurred with regards to the location of POEs. Judges in counties without POEs ordered defendants to pay an overall average of 68.4 percent of original fines while those cases heard in counties with POEs were assessed an average of only 58.9 percent of the original fine.

These results reject the hypotheses that judges in smaller counties and counties without POEs diminish the importance of

Table 4.   Total Citations Issued, Total Funds Collectible (on All Cases)
and Collected, Average Percent of Original Fine Paid
on All Cases and Contested Cases in Each County

County	Total Citations Issued	Amount Collected ($)	Avg. Percent of Original Fine Paid (All Cases)	Avg. Percent of Original Fine Paid (Contested Cases)
BENTON	334	54,776	80	45
CLARK	2,173	373,104	85	57
GRAYS HARBOR	552	88,773	86	67
KING	1,905	347,853	83	70
KITTITAS	802	135,017	91	74
PIERCE	966	149,575	79	58
SKAGIT	1,281	298,704	89	82
SPOKANE	391	89,570	92	70
WALLA WALLA[a]	184	26,376	61	58
STUDY TOTAL	8,588	1,563,748	85	66

Note: [a] There were some citations reported being issued in either Benton or Walla Walla counties (actual county was not specified); those citations were divided equally between the two counties for the "Total Citations Issued" category.

overweight violations and greatly reduce fines. For all cases in the data set, court location had little influence on the amount of the original fine that was collected. However, for the contested cases ruled guilty, a relationship did exist between court location and fine difference. The courts located in counties with populations over 100,000 tended to have judges who lowered fines to a greater degree than those counties with smaller numbers of residents. This may be a result of lack of education or interest in commercial vehicle weight rules and regulations. Judges in larger counties where violent crimes occur frequently may award precedence to such crimes in the courtroom. This could ultimately result in large reductions on fines for offenses some judges may see as "trivial," including violating truck weight limits.

Defendant's Address

Addresses of defendants were examined to determine whether the location of residence (of the driver) had an effect on fine difference. In Washington, if fines are not paid by the due date,

Washington operators' licenses are suspended. There is a reciprocal agreement between Washington and Oregon which allows each state to suspend the other's residents' licenses as well as their own. For those defendants residing in one of the remaining 48 states or Canada, no such recourse can be taken. An out-of-state letter may be sent demanding payment, or collection agencies may be utilized to collect the outstanding balances. Due to these regulations, defendants from out-of-state and Canada should probably have higher numbers of unsettled cases than those from Washington and Oregon. Moreover, the punitive rate for out-of-state and Canadian residents should be higher than those for Washington and Oregon residents because out-of-state and Canadian residents are more likely to pay the ticket than return to Washington to contest it in court, especially if they plan to travel through Washington in the future.

The percent of original fine paid on all cases by defendants' addresses is depicted in Figure 5. Canadian residents paid an average of 99.5 percent of the original fine on all cases and out-of-state residents paid an average of 93.4 percent of original fines. Those defendants residing in Washington and Oregon paid an average of 83.2 percent and 80 percent of the original fines on all cases. This does support the inference that those defendants who live in Canada or a state other than Washington and Oregon tend to pay their tickets rather than return to Washington to contest their case in court.

The relationship between address of defendant and the punitive rate for contested cases was similar to that of paid cases (Figure 6). Canadian residents paid the highest average, 98 percent of the original fine. A majority of these (88 percent) were identified as contested because defendants failed to respond to the court within the allotted time. After notices informing defendants of their failure to respond were issued by the courts, tickets were often paid in full, resulting in 100 percent of the original fine being paid on a contested case. Out-of-state residents paid an average of 59 percent and Oregon residents paid an average of 47 percent. These numbers suggest that some judges may be more reluctant to lower fines on violations committed by defendants from out-of-state and Canada, or tend to be more lenient with Washington and Oregon

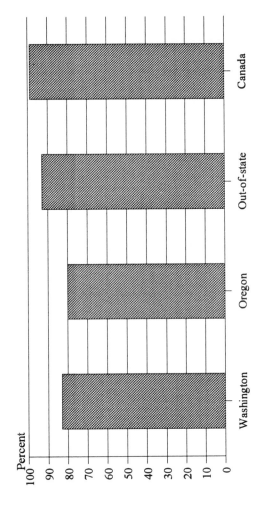

Figure 5. Percent of Original Fine Paid on All Cases by Defendant's Address

150

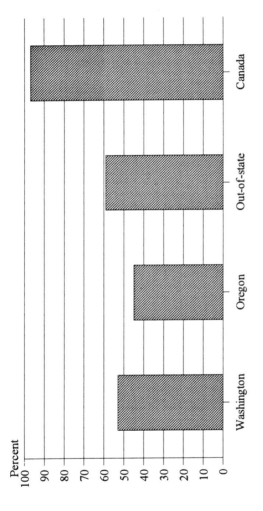

Figure 6. Percent of Original Fine Paid on Contested Cases

residents. Thus, the effective punitive rate (γ) for Washington and Oregon residents is considerably lower than that for out-of-state and Canadian residents. This may be another explanation as to the high percentage of Washington and Oregon residents that contest their cases compared to those from Canada and out-of-state. While defendants from Washington and Oregon tend to contest cases, those from out-of-state and Canada frequently pay their tickets. However, Canadian and out-of-state residents are more frequently involved in neglecting to pay or contest their tickets, thus becoming parties in unsettled cases. Due partly to the Washington/Oregon reciprocal agreement regarding driver's license suspension, the residents of these two states are more apt to settle their cases than those who live out-of-state and in Canada.

Violation Magnitude

A positive correlation is obviously expected between excess weight and fine amount. Fines for very heavy trucks can be costly and may mean those caught with excessive overloads are more apt to contest their citations than those with·lesser fines. Most violations were in the 0 to 2.4 *Kip* (*Kip* = 1,000 pounds) overweight category and most (68.8 percent) of those tickets were paid. As excess weight increased, there was an increase in the percentage of contested cases versus paid cases. This suggests that truckers who have tickets with large penalties believe they can get the fine reduced if their case is heard before a judge. With the lower fines it may be more efficient to pay the ticket rather than take the time and effort to contest it in court. This illustrates how the trucker's economic incentive to overload is influenced through the punitive (γ) rate. If the trucker realizes that contesting the case will result in some fine reduction, the incentive to the trucker is to contest overweight violations, especially for large overweight violations where the initial penalty may exceed the economic benefit from overloading.

The punitive rate does vary with the magnitude of excess weights. The percent of original fine paid for all cases decreased as excess weight increased. Exceptions were found in the 12.5 to 14.9 *Kip* overweight group which also had a larger percentage of

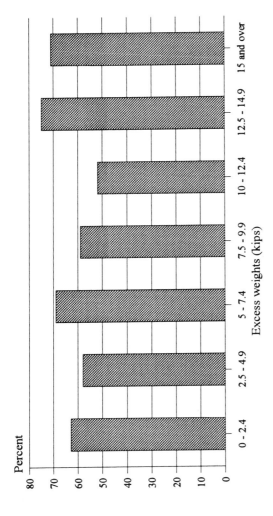

Figure 7. Percent of Original Fine Paid on Guilty Cases for Various Excess Weights

153

contested cases. The percentage of contested cases in the heavier
excess weight categories increased generally. Similarly, larger fines
were reduced to a greater degree than the smaller fines, generally,
for all cases. However, for contested cases this wasn't true. The
two largest percent of original fines paid on contested cases
occurred in the 12.5 to 14.9 *Kip* and 15 and oover *Kip* excess weight
categories where an average of 76.4 percent and 71.2 percent of
the original fines were paid, respectively (Figure 7). Results suggest
that some judges realize the very heavy trucks are causing immense
damage to pavements and feel that violators should be held
financially accountable.

Response

As previously mentioned, a ticket on an overweight violation
can either be paid or contested in court. The way truckers respond
should have a noticeable effect on percent of original fine paid.
Tickets that are paid constitute 100 percent of the original fine,
while contested tickets result in fines that vary between 0 and 100
percent of the original assessment. The punitive rate on all
contested cases was 56.3 percent. This included averages of 63
percent on 220 cases found guilty, 14 percent on one amended case,
2 percent on 19 dismissed cases, and 0 percent on seven cases found
not guilty.

The 63 percent on guilty cases illustrates that 37 percent of
potential revenue from contested cases found guilty is being "lost"
in the court system. Judges more often assessed penalties in the
range of 61-70 percent of the original fine than in any other decile
(Figure 8). The next most frequent decile were 41-50 percent and
91-100 percent, illustrating that some judges are lenient while
others are stringent when it comes to assessing penalties for weight
violations. Thus, the courts' effectiveness varies by the degree of
excess weight which could have implications concerning
educational efforts aimed at improving their effectiveness.

Often reductions in fines reflect circumstances surrounding the
case and may not be avoided. However, in some cases, fines are
reduced to a token of their original amount for reasons many law
enforcement officers, in interviews, considered unjust. While the

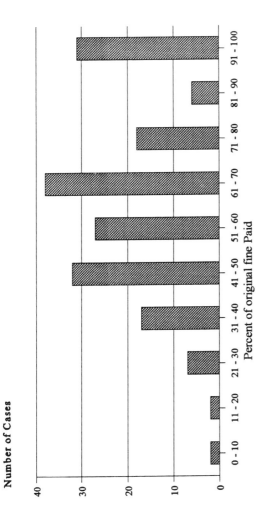

Figure 8. Percent of Original Fine Paid on Guilty Cases

155

fine for a non-contested paid response is always 100 percent, the percentage of statutory penalty actually enforced by a court will tend to vary for a contested response depending on evidence and the trial judge inclinations.

C. Fine Collections

Average original fines were computed for each possible disposition. The one Amended case had a fine of $332.00 while the averages of the four other dispositions were as follows: Dismissed = $295.00; Not Guilty = $288.00; Guilty = $236.00; and Paid = $198.00. The total number of citations issued between September 1991 and August 1992 was 10,388. Therefore, the total amount of assessments collected during the sample period was $2.2 million, based on dispositions as a percentage of total cases (See Figure 3) and the average original fines shown above. Paid cases reflected 100 percent of the original fine so $1,302,048 was collected on paid dispositions. There were 36 unsettled cases which were classified as guilty (through hearings and failure to respond). They were used in the calculation of average original fines for cases with guilty dispositions; however, they are separated into an individual category for this analysis. The maximum collectable amount on the unsettled cases was $130,036. None of that money had been collected as of January 1, 1993. Sixty-three percent ($247,639) of the total possible $669,296 was collected on contested cases. Only 2 percent ($1,374) of the possible $68,676 was paid on cases that were dismissed while all the $29,952 of charges on cases that were found not guilty was dropped and thus not collected. The amended case was charged an average of 14 percent of the original fine resulting in $976 being collected from the possible $5,996. The total civil assessments collected during the year was $1,801,005 or 82 percent of the maximum possible.

VI.   CONCLUSIONS

Roads and highways across the nation are subject to accelerated deterioration from overloaded trucks, operating with and without appropriate weight permits. The number of overweight trucks on roads and highways, and thus the rate of accelerated highway deterioration, is predominately influenced by the fee/fine (permit) system, the capture rate (α) of illegally operated trucks and the judges' decision involving individual overweight infractions (punitive rate). This study identifies how the trucker's economic incentive to overload is influenced by changes in the punitive rate and provides a case study of Washington's fine system in recapturing the physical and eventual financial damage from overloaded vehicles, through the court and legal process. The firm's decision to overload trucks (their choice of "Q" in maximizing profits in Equation 1) is directly influenced by both capture and punitive rates. Affecting the trucker's incentive to overload may require utilizing these "instruments" to obtain the desired outcome. Specifically, the punitive rate (γ) was evaluated through the percent of original fine paid on overweight citations, in addition to relationships such as weight, fine amount, type of response, court location and defendants address.

Between September 1991 and August 1992 there were 10,388 overweight citations issued. As of January 1, 1993 only 82 percent of the possible total civil assessment of $2.2 million was collected. The average percent of original fine paid (punitive rate) on contested cases was 56.3 with the average percent of original fine paid on guilty cases being 63 percent. Thus, 37 percent of potential revenue from guilty cases is being "lost" in the court system. The loss in state and local revenue is further exemplified by the fact that judges most frequently assign fines which are only 61-70 percent of the original fine value. Combined with the decrease in revenues is the increased incentive to truckers to overload given the conceptual relationship defined earlier between the quantity per truckload and the capture rate (α) and punitive rate (γ). Decreases in either rate will increase the incentive to load trucks to their maximum physical payload. Results from this analysis indicate an increase in the number of contested cases as the magnitude of truck overload increases, illustrating how fine reductions increase overloading activity.

Surprisingly, smaller counties and counties without POEs had higher punitive rates on contested cases than the larger counties

158   ERIC L. JESSUP

and those with POEs. This result rejects the hypothesis that judges in smaller counties and counties without POEs are more lenient on overweight violations and drastically reduce overweight fines. The reluctance of judges from smaller counties to decrease overweight fines could stem from the way the fee and fine system is structured. Specifically, the 57 percent of revenue from overweight violations distributed to local government is a larger proportion of the total budget for local governments in smaller counties than it is for larger counties which have larger tax bases and more revenue sources.

The results presented in this study do provide an evaluation of how effective this state's court and legal process are in recovering road damage through fine enforcement. A significant portion of fine revenues (18%) are lost in the court system, particularly from contested cases (37%) which are found guilty but have fines reduced. The are several strategies which can be used to address this problem, in Washington and throughout the United States.

If the loss in potential fine revenues creates a situation where road and highway damage is greater than net fee/fine revenues then one method of addressing the imbalance is to simply utilize the findings of this study to educate and inform state lawmakers. A greater understanding of how overweight fines are affected by the courts and legal processes will enable lawmakers to develop state statutes which consider the fact net fines are less than 100 percent of their original value. Raising the fees and/or fines for overloading would decrease the incentive to overload while also increasing the net revenue per permit and citation. Additionally, law enforcement efforts devoted to overload violations could be strengthened to increase the capture rate, thus decreasing the incentive to overload while providing increased fine revenues.

A more direct, and possibly more effective, approach to addressing the problem of exaggerated fine reductions is to utilize the information provided in this study to target judicial educational efforts. If judges are better informed about the intent and purpose of the overweight fines (to serve as both deterrent and recapture of financial road damage) they may be less likely to reduce overweight fines on a regular basis. A cost-effective allocation of this nature may allow enforcement officials and district judges to realize the importance of the percent of original fine paid and its relationship to the capture rate (violation rate) and the resultant damage to the state's roads and highways.

ACKNOWLEDGMENTS

Appreciation is expressed to the Commercial Vehicle Enforcement Officers of the Washington State Patrol, especially Captain Richard F. Randolph for cooperation and assistance in providing the data and to Catherine Barron for data collection and assimilation. Appreciation is also expressed to Professor Ken Casavant at Washington State University for his valuable expertise and advise.

REFERENCES

Barron, C.J., Jessup, E.L., & Casavant, K.L. (1994, July). *A case study of the effectiveness of Washington's fine system for overweight violations.* Final Technical Report, Washington State Department of Transportation.

Casavant, K.L. (1991a, September). WA-RD 242.1: *A preliminary evaluation of the equity of the truck fee and fine system in Washington.* Olympia, WA: Washington State Department of Transportation.

Casavant, K.L. (1991b, September). WA-RD 242.2: *1991 state fee and fine regulations for overweight vehicles: A national survey.* Olympia, WA: Washington State Department of Transportation.

Jessup, E.L., & Casavant, K.L. (1995, September). *Estimation of violation and capture of overweight trucks: A case study.* Final Technical Report, Washington State Department of Transportation.

R.C.W. 46.44. (1991). *West's revised code of Washington annotated and 1992 cumulative annual pocket part.* St. Paul, MN: West Publishing Company.

T.R.B. (Transportation Research Board). (1987, September). National Cooperative Highway Research Program Synthesis 131: *Effects of permit and illegal overloads on pavements.* Washington, DC: National Research Council.

Washington State Patrol. (1989-1993). *State of Washington: certification of size and weight enforcement.* 23 CFR 657.13, Annual Reports.

J
A
I

Research in
Transportation Economics

Edited by **B. Starr McMullen,** *Department of Economics, Oregon State University*

Volume 3, 1994, 176 pp. $73.25
ISBN 0-89232-691-3

CONTENTS: Preface, *B. Starr McMullen.* Network Connectivity and Price Convergence: Gas Pipeline Deregulation, *Arthur De Vany and W. David Walls.* Deregulation of U.S. Airlines and Motor Carriers: A Model of Industry Equilibrium and Consumer Welfare, *Dong Liu.* Nonprice Competition, Cost Shocks, and Profitability in the Airline Industry, *Messod D. Beneish and Michael J. Moore.* Motor Bus Driver Earnings in Regulated and Deregulated Environments, *Ann Schwarrz-Miller and Wayne K. Talley.* The Economic Impact of Alternative Rail Pricing Schemes, *Victor E. Eusebio, Stephen J. Rindom, and Ali Abderrezak.* TRANSPORTATION ISSUES. Light Rail and Bus Priority Systems: Choice or Blind Commitment?, *David A. Hensher and WIliam G. Waters II.*

Also Available:
Volumes 1-2 (1983-1985) $73.25 each

P
R
E
S
S

FACULTY/PROFESSIONAL discounts are available in the U.S. and Canada at a rate of 40% off the list price when prepaid by personal check or credit card and ordered directly from the publisher.

JAI PRESS INC.
55 Old Post Road No. 2 - P.O. Box 1678
Greenwich, Connecticut 06836-1678
Tel: (203) 661- 7602   Fax: (203) 661-0792

Research in Urban Economics

Edited by **R. D. Norton,** *Sarkisian Professor of Business Economics, Bryant College*

Volume 10, New Urban Strategies in Advanced Regional Economies
1996, 248 pp. $73.25
ISBN 1-55938-856-0

REVIEW: "... this volume contains a wealth of information that shed much light on various urban phenomena, and should therefore prove very helpful to both students and researchers ..."
— *Annals of Regional Science*

CONTENTS: Introduction: Re-Thinking City Economic Development, *R.D. Norton.* The High Price of High Costs, *Mark Zandi.* Out-Migration as Adjustment in New England, *Edward J. Deak and Philip J. Lane.* World Cities: New York's Struggle to Stay on Top, *Ann R. Markusen and Vicky Gwiasda.* The Changing Industrial Structure of the New York Region, *Matthew P. Drennan.* U.S. Computing's Westward Reinvigoration, *R.D. Norton.* Transportation Policy and the 1990 Clean Air Act, *Alvaro E. Pereira and Karen R. Polenske.* Boston's Big Dig: Pump-Priming as Urban Policy, *Kenneth M. Mead.* SME's and Regional Economic Development, *Niles M. Hansen.* Urban Entrepreneurialism and National Economic Growth, *Henry G. Cisneros.* Appedix: Economic Development Literature in the 1990s—Abstracts and Annotations.

Also Available:
Volumes 1-9 (1981-1993) $73.25 each

J
A
I

P
R
E
S
S

JAI PRESS INC.
55 Old Post Road No. 2 - P.O. Box 1678
Greenwich, Connecticut 06836-1678
Tel: (203) 661- 7602   Fax: (203) 661-0792

J A I

P R E S S

Research in Real Estate

Edited by **Steven D. Kapplin** and **Arthur L. Schwartz, Jr.**, *Department of Finance, University of South Florida*

Volume 3, 1990, 261 pp. $73.25
ISBN 0-89232-422-8

CONTENTS: Introduction. Shanties as Real Estate: Analyzing Markets in the Making, *Saad Yahya and Nicky Nzioki*. The Role of Visual Presence in The Urban Office Location and Office Market Behavior, *Wayne R. Archer, Marc T. Smith, and Dean H. Gatzlaff*. Enhancing the Quality of Real Estate Decisions by Use of the Judgmental Model, *Maury Seldin and John Hysom*. The Contribution of Demographic Methods to Real Estate Market Analysis, *Dowell Myers*. Analyzing Real Estate Asset Performance During Periods of Market Disequilibrium Under Cyclical Economic Conditions: A Framework for Analysis, *Stephen A. Pyhrr, James R. Webb, and Waldo L. Born*. Systematic Biases in Housing Market Analysis, *Dowell Myers*. Real Estate Market Analysis: Application of Data and Techniques to a Case Study, *Waldo L. Born*. Appendix A: Market Research Publications Section, *Waldo L. Born*. Appendix B: Online Database Information Section, *Waldo L. Born*.

Also Available:
Volumes 1-2 (1982) $73.25 each

FACULTY/PROFESSIONAL discounts are available in the U.S. and Canada at a rate of 40% off the list price when prepaid by personal check or credit card and ordered directly from the publisher.

JAI PRESS INC.
55 Old Post Road No. 2 - P.O. Box 1678
Greenwich, Connecticut 06836-1678
Tel: (203) 661- 7602   Fax: (203) 661-0792

Research in Labor Economics

Edited by **Solomon W. Polachek,** *Department of Economics, State University of New York, Binghamton*

Volume 15, 1996, 392 pp. $78.50
ISBN 0-7623-0111-2

CONTENTS: Preface, *Solomon W. Polachek.* Growth and Labor Mobility, *Yoram Weiss.* The Effects of Minimum Wages on Teenage Employment and Enrollment: Evidence from Matched CPS Surveys, *David Neumark and William Wascher.* Public Policies and the Working Poor: The Earned Income Tax Credit Versus Minimum Wage Legislation, *Richard V. Burkhauser, Kenneth A. Couch, and Andrew J. Glenn.* The Structure and Consequences of Eligibility Rules for a Social Program: A Study of Job Training Partnership Act (JTPA), *Theresa J. Devine and James J. Heckman.* Testing Job Search Models: The Laboratory Approach, *James C. Cox and Ronald L. Oaxaca.* An Econometric Analysis of the Demand for Private Schooling, *Barry R. Chiswick and Stella Koutromanes.* Does It Pay to Attend an Elite Private College? Evidence from the Senior High School Class of 1980, *Dominic J. Brewer and Ronald G. Ehrenberg.* Employer Size and Labor Turnover, *Todd L. Idson.* Unions and Productivity in the Public Sector: The Case of Sanitation Workers, *Linda N. Edwards and Elizabeth Field-Hendrey.* Evaluating Mental Health Capitation Treatment: Lessons from Panel Data, *Debra Sabatini Dwyer, Olivia S. Mitchell, Robert Cole, and Sylvia K. Reed.* An Event Analysis of Female Labor Supply, *Alice Nakamura and Masao Nakamura.*

Also Available:
Volumes 1-14 (1977-1995)
  + Supplements 1-2 (1979-1983) $78.50 each

JAI PRESS INC.
55 Old Post Road No. 2 - P.O. Box 1678
Greenwich, Connecticut 06836-1678
Tel: (203) 661- 7602   Fax: (203) 661-0792

J
A
I

P
R
E
S
S

Advances in the Economics of Energy and Resources

Edited by **John R. Moroney,** *Department of Economics, Texas A&M University*

Volume 9, Sustainable Economic Growth
1995, 241 pp. $78.50
ISBN 1-55938-922-2

CONTENTS: Introduction, *John R. Moroney.* Economic Sustainability, *John R. Moroney.* Fossil Fuel Use and Sustainable Development: Evidence from U.S. Input-Output Data, 1972-1985, *Richard W. England and Stephen D. Casler.* Sustainable Growth and Valuation of Mineral Reserves, *M.A. Adelman.* Commentary, *Teofilo Ozuna.* Economic Conservation Policy: Implications for Economic Growth and Consumer Welfare, *Donald A. Norman.* Commentary, *Jeff Talbert.* U.S. Petroleum Supply: History and Prospects, *Edward D. Porter.* Commentary, *Bryan Maggard.* Trends in U.S. Natural Gas Production, *Robert A. Wattenbarger and Mauricio Villegas.* Commentary, *James Griffin.* Distributional and Environmental Consequences of Taxes on Energy, *Hadi Dowlatabadi, Raymond J. Kopp and F. Ted Tschang.* Commentary, *M. Douglas Berg.*

Also Available:

Volumes 1-8 (1979-1994)
+ Supplement 1 (1994) $73.25 each

JAI PRESS INC.
55 Old Post Road No. 2 - P.O. Box 1678
Greenwich, Connecticut 06836-1678
Tel: (203) 661- 7602   Fax: (203) 661-0792